Helplessness and Hope

BRUCE D. RUMBOLD

Helplessness and Hope

Pastoral Care in Terminal Illness

SCM PRESS LTD

British Library Cataloguing in Publication Data.

Rumbold, Bruce D.
Helplessness and hope: pastoral care in
terminal illness.
1. Terminal care——Religious aspects——
Christianity
I. Title
261.8'32175   R726.8

ISBN 0–334–02045–X

First published 1986
by SCM Press Ltd
26–30 Tottenham Road, London N1

Phototypeset by Input Typesetting Ltd, London
and Printed in Great Britain by
Richard Clay (The Chaucer Press) plc
Bungay, Suffolk

To my father
Charles David Rumbold
1905–1980
and my father-in-law
Donald Reay Dyer
1922–1983

CONTENTS

INTRODUCTION

What I am attempting in this book is an overview of terminal care from a pastoral perspective. Part of the book is devoted to making explicit what I mean by this; but in summary form I understand pastoral care to be care of a whole person in the context of his or her community. Thus pastoral care has a common area of concern with all other forms of care, but is interested particularly in how the various dimensions of care – physical, social, emotional and spiritual – hold together. A specific pastoral concern is that the spiritual dimension be explored alongside other aspects of care.

This broad pastoral perspective undergirds the whole book. At times it is implicit while discussion is carried on in terms of other disciplinary perspectives. At other times it is made explicit in an attempt to clarify some of the assessments made and directions pursued. Sometimes it may seem that there are two books intermingled here. I trust that this will not be the final impression. My intention is both to offer a critique of terminal care and to expose and discuss the values by which this critique is made. Hopefully those who read the book from a pastoral background will be stimulated to reflect upon how their pastoral practice might be grounded in the world of practical terminal care, while those who read from the perspective of another helping discipline will be encouraged to reflect on the values which underlie their approach to care.

Thus the book is addressed to people interested in terminal care, particularly those practising in the area in either a professional or volunteer capacity. It is not intended simply for religious caring people, although a religious dimension of care is integral to what I have to say. It is not a book which develops strategies for care in great detail, although I hope that it is practical enough to aid in developing and assessing such strategies. Thus it is not intended as a self-help guide, the sort of book you read when faced with your own dying or with looking after a dying parent, spouse, child or friend. It is a more general reflection on terminal care and its place in our society.

The book has its origins in work undertaken in the Department of Social and Pastoral Theology in the University of Manchester. The material presented here has been developed further through my involvement in care of dying people, terminal care training and discussions with a variety of people, professional and lay, during nine years of parish ministry in Melbourne, Australia.

I have learned from and been encouraged by many people, including those who have shared their dying with me. There are some people, however, whom I would want to acknowledge specifically here. My supervisors in the University of Manchester, Professor Ronald Preston and Canon Frank Wright, gave great support and encouragement during the two years I lived in Manchester, and since that time Ronald Preston has continued to encourage me in writing. My community, the members of the Box Hill Baptist Church, have been generous and supportive over many years, and I am most grateful to them. I would like to thank friends among them who have read and commented upon sections of this manuscript. They are not responsible for the shortcomings of the final product, but they have contributed significantly to whatever clarity and balance it has. Especially I would want to thank my wife Jean for her constructive criticism, encouragement and support throughout the writing of this book.

I

· *Terminal Care Today* ·

The last sixty years have seen a major change in the way we die. Life expectancy in the industrialized Western nations has increased from fifty-five years in 1915 to over seventy years at the present time. Leaving aside the staggering number of deaths resulting from war and the aftermath of war, the major causes of death in this century have changed from acute infectious illnesses to degenerative illnesses, principally cancer and cardiovascular disease. With this change, the mortality of younger age groups, and of children in particular, has fallen dramatically. The location of death too has changed. At the turn of the century only about 10% of deaths occurred in institutions. Now it is around 80% in the United States, a comparable figure in Australia, and about 65% in the United Kingdom. Most of us can expect to die at a relatively advanced age, from a degenerative condition which will warn us (if we wish to be warned) of our impending death. And we will probably die in an institution, our primary care in the hands of professional helpers, our family and friends becoming occasional visitors rather than companions in our last days of life.

Another outcome of these changes is that a personal encounter with death, in the sense of losing a family member or close friend, is now relatively rare prior to adulthood. Even then, the actual event of death is remote from most adults' experience, as dying people are usually institutionalized in the terminal phase of illness. The deaths of people we know and love are distanced from our lives; and with this distancing we become less prepared to deal with death when it arises within our personal sphere. Distancing both reinforces and results from what has been called our denial of death; our apparent unwillingness to consider death as a reality for us personally. This phrase 'denial of death' has become something of a cliché in describing contemporary attitudes to death. In so far as it implies that there is an overall social attitude, it is incorrect. Rather, the evidence available to us from various surveys is that there is *no* common social attitude to death. The American sociologist Talcott Parsons contends that what we have interpreted as denial is in reality a kind of apathy: confronted by death we do not know what to do or say, and so we minimize any overt expression or action.[1] Thus a personal encounter with death is something we avoid when we can, and try to cope with when we must. Because our usual policy is avoidance, and because we have no clear-cut social attitudes to guide us, our resources for coping are limited. It suits us to perceive dying essentially as a medical problem, so that a hospital becomes the appropriate place to die, with the companions of the dying being the professionals involved in the 'management of terminal disease'.

This new style of dying confronts us with a number of questions. How do dying people and their families cope in the (frequently lengthy) period of illness preceding death? How does institutional care affect them? How do professional helpers deal with the almost-total responsibility for care for dying people which is given to them by the rest of society? How, in the absence of any general social meaning for death, can a dying person find meaning? And coming closer to home: how best can I care for a dying person? How can I die well? To consider the questions we need first to take a closer look at the experiences of dying and of caring for dying people.

The experience of dying

Dying has become a popular subject for discussion and investigation largely through the efforts of Elisabeth Kübler-Ross. While foundations were laid by work on both sides of the Atlantic in the 1950s and '60s, it is Dr Ross' description of the dying process, based on interviews with over four hundred terminally ill patients in the University of Chicago Billings Hospital, which is cited throughout the contemporary literature on dying.[2]

Kübler-Ross suggests that dying people pass through a series of five stages from the initial shock of discovering their prognosis to final acceptance of their death. Moving out of the initial shock, a dying person begins to express feelings of guilt, anxiety and anger. This phase is followed by one in which the reality of illness is admitted, but the dying person tries consciously or unconsciously to affect the outcome by bargaining with a person or influence who is seen to be in control of the situation ('If only I do everything which the doctor suggests, then perhaps I will recover.' 'If only I pray and read my Bible then surely God will spare me. . .') Bargaining gives way to depression as the inevitability of death is realized. Finally a stable attitude of acceptance can be reached as the person discovers a meaning in dying. In schematic form these stages are:

1. Denial and isolation (*Not me!*)
2. Anger (and partial denial) (*Why me?*)
3. Bargaining (*Perhaps me, but...*)
4. Depression (*It is me*)
5. Acceptance and preparatory grief

Kübler-Ross is careful to stress that these stages are not to be taken too literally. They are a general description; the stages overlap, and the time an individual spends in a particular stage may vary between a few minutes and several months. A further important factor in a dying person's movement from shock and denial to acceptance is the availability of someone to whom the dying person can freely express his or her feelings and thoughts. If no such person is available, the emotional work of dying will be retarded drastically.

Elisabeth Kübler-Ross' work has been of great value in understanding and helping dying people. Her emphasis is on the possibility of a person finding meaning and fulfilment in dying, and this emphasis is having a far-reaching effect on the type and quality of care offered to people dying in hospitals. Nevertheless, the simplicity of her model has lent itself to abuse, particularly by people who persist in using it diagnostically ('This person is in Stage 2, and so our responses will be...'), thus failing to perceive the person in the patient.

Another scheme has been put forward by a co-worker of Kübler-Ross, Carl Nighswonger, Chaplain in Billings Hospital. Nighswonger's description has two major advantages. The first is that he places less emphasis on stages by postulating a series of dramas in which a dying person may find himself involved. These dramas are in some respects similar to the Kübler-Ross stages, but Nighswonger develops them to show that a dying person is not just immersed in one attitude at one particular stage. Rather, he is working at the options which are before him. Will he admit the devastating news of his dying into consciousness, and risk falling to pieces in panic; or will he block it out in denial? Will he express his anger and guilt; or will he push it under in depression? Nighswonger's scheme is as follows:[3]

Drama of Shock:	denial v. panic
Emotion:	catharsis v. depression
Negotiation:	bargaining v. surrendering
Assessment:	realistic hope v. despair

Commitment: acceptance v. resignation
Completion: fulfillment v. forlornness

Nighswonger's model thus displays two parallel sequences of possible attitudes. One, like the Kübler-Ross stages, leads to a point of acceptance and fulfilment in dying; the other leads to resignation and forlornness. The presence of this alternative path with its endpoint in forlornness is Nighswonger's second major contribution. It makes explicit a fact which the Kübler-Ross model could handle only by postulating an incomplete dying process: the fact that many people die alone, stoically resigned to their fate. Positive acceptance or affirmation of death is not the only endpoint in dying. Hope and meaning are not necessarily achieved. Indeed, depression and resignation seem to be much more common than affirmation and acceptance in the face of death.

The Nighswonger model also makes for greater clarity in understanding the way environment may affect a dying person's attitudes. The context of home or hospital, and the network of relationships involving a dying person, will tend to reinforce one or other option in each of the dramas. Thus the environment may assist a dying person to resolve her feelings and attitudes; or it may perpetuate a struggle in which the dying person is unable to give full expression to her feelings because of her situation and the attitudes of the people around her. Environment can be a very important factor in whether a dying person's choices keep her on the road to acceptance and fulfilment, or move her into the negative trajectory leading to despair and forlornness.

While such models of the dying process can lead to very useful insights, it is important to be aware of some possible limitations. For a start, much research into dying is based around 'interesting cases', people who for one reason or another have attracted the researcher's attention.[4] Kübler-Ross's model is open to question at this point. It is based on interviews with patients selected because of their verbal ability and their willingness to share their experience in teaching sessions involving a variety of helping professionals. Such people are by no means typical. Because of this, helping strategies based on the Kübler-Ross model may not always be appropriate. When a dying person has few verbal or conceptual skills, the role of helper is less likely to be that of a sympathetic interpreter facilitating movement towards acceptance: more time will be spent sustaining, directing, giving reassurance, perhaps even supporting defences which the helper sees as less than healthy or ideal.[5]

A second qualification of these models is that they give a description which focusses solely on the dying person. To make such a description the basis for a model of terminal care is not enough. Any protracted terminal illness involves a number of people; family, friends and professional helpers as well as the dying person. Everyone involved will be making some sort of adjustment to the situation 'this person is dying'. The interaction of these different adjustment processes is complex. It certainly is not enough to single out the dying person and consider only his or her needs, neglecting the attitudes and needs of family, friends and professional helpers. It is to a consideration of these attitudes and needs that we now turn.

The experience of family and friends

When a person is diagnosed as terminally-ill, friends and family are faced with the imminent loss of someone who has been a significant part of their lives. Being confronted in this way with the certainty of personal loss requires adjustment, and family and friends must start on a process of realizing the news and facing a future without the person who is now dying. The first response is usually shock and denial, which gives way to emotional turmoil as the reality of the situation comes home, until finally some measure of acceptance is achieved. This process is in fact very similar to the dying person's preparatory grief. However, the path is usually easier for family and friends. They are more likely to have opportunities to discuss the situation openly with each other and with medical staff. Also, for them the impending loss, while life-changing, is less absolute than the finality of physical death facing the dying person.

Recent studies of family responses use the term 'anticipatory grief' to describe this process of realization and adjustment. Anticipatory grief is very similar to the grief of bereavement, although it cannot replace the grieving which must be done once the person dies. But if family and friends are able to grieve in anticipation, they will be better prepared for the person's death when it occurs, and they will be able to cope better with their bereavement.[6] Difficulties arise, however, if the family's anticipatory grief and the dying person's preparatory grief proceed independently. If, for example, the dying person has begun to accept death, but the family insists on maintaining denial and will not accept the new perspective, the dying person can become very isolated. Isolation can also be the result if the dying person lingers long after the family has worked through its anticipatory grief and begun to function as a social unit which no longer requires the dying person; the person is dead socially even if not yet physically. Ideally,

Kutscher suggests, anticipatory grief and grief in bereavement should be seen as a continuum, and anticipatory grief should be linked with the dying person's preparatory grief.[7]

For this ideal to be realized, there must be open communication between all involved in the situation. This state of affairs is not easily achieved, particularly if the dying person is hospitalized. Too often an institution seems to immobilize a family. Sometimes open communication is inhibited by a doctor's directive that 'the patient must not know'. Even if this is not the case an unfamiliar environment, lack of real privacy, perhaps carefully-controlled visiting hours, all have their effect. Added to this is the covert message implied by the hospital taking total responsibility for patient care. This sort of care might include, for example, an elderly woman being sent out of the ward while a junior nurse washes or gives an injection to the man to whom she has been married for fifty years. There may of course be good reasons for a policy like this, but that is hardly the point. It is little wonder that some family members receive a message that the patient is now the hospital's property, and that sometimes they need to be given explicit permission just to sit with, touch, or caress a dying relative.

Yet to place all blame on the hospital staff for this state of affairs would be unjust. The conspiracy of silence about death is a social phenomenon, not a professional invention.[8] All of us are culpable to some degree. Whilst the institutional structure can create severe difficulties for patients and families, it must also be recognized that the structure itself is created by the attitudes and needs of hospital staff as they seek to deal with the overwhelming burden of death and bereavement delegated to them by society. The hospital reflects, as well as influences, society's attitudes to illness and dying.[9]

The experience of hospital staff

Many of the comments made in the literature about the attitudes of medical staff to dying patients are inferred from observing staff behaviour rather than by direct conversation or investigation. As such, the comments rely heavily on the observer's interpretation of this behaviour. However, several studies have attempted quantitative assessment of doctors' or nurses' attitudes to death using psychological measurement tests. One such study, comparing the attitudes of physicians, medical students, terminally-ill people and healthy individuals, found that the physicians were significantly more afraid of death, and of dying in particular, than the other three groups. Medical students' attitudes were in the middle ground between the physicians and the other two groups, healthy and terminally-ill individuals without medical training. There was no significant difference in attitude between the latter two groups.[10]

On the basis of these findings, which are supported by other studies, the researchers suggested that an above-average fear of death may be an important unconscious factor in selecting a medical career in the first place. Such a phenomenon is of course not confined to medical career choices; a component in vocational choice for many people is a desire to achieve competence or mastery in a field which both fascinates and troubles them. It is particularly true of the helping professions. But if factors like this are operative, it implies that physicians have a strong personal investment in controlling disease in other people. Inability to do so, represented particularly by a patient's death, is a failure of this control. Helplessness in the face of death is thus an acutely painful experience for many doctors. It threatens both their sense of professional competence and their personal identity, for identity is closely bound up with professional performance.

Data directly comparing nurses' attitudes with those of doctors are not available, but studies seem to indicate that similar dynamics operate for nurses, who also show above-average death anxiety.[11]

Thus while the attention given to professional helpers' attitudes has been nothing like that devoted to studies of dying people and their families, the available data certainly challenge some basic assumptions about medical care during terminal illness. One such assumption is that medically-trained personnel are the people best equipped to care for dying persons. While this assumption is valid in the area of technical physical care, it is not necessarily valid for emotional aspects of care. The evidence indicates that, if anything, professional helpers have fewer innate emotional resources for providing terminal care than the average lay person; yet society gives almost the whole emotional burden of terminal care to medical personnel. A second questionable assumption is implied in much of the medical literature on terminal care. Here the patients' behaviour is usually regarded as psychologically determined by their predicament, while staff are assumed to be free of such constraints, able to adopt whichever attitude is most appropriate for the well-being of the patients. This assumption is clearly incorrect, and the ways in which the attitudes and defences of staff, patients and families interact requires much more attention.

Dying in an institution

Most deaths nowadays occur in hospitals or nursing homes. Even when people die at home, they will often have spent a considerable proportion of their last months or years of life in hospital or in an institution run along hospital lines. As the place of death has moved from home to institution, hospitals have had to find ways of dealing with the differing perspectives and needs of all those involved in a terminal illness. The needs and desires of patients, families and friends, and professional helpers are not altogether compatible, and decisions must be made about which needs will be met, which set aside. Some of these decisions can be worked out in the particular situation; but many more have already been made and built into institutional structures.

Institutions develop in order to carry out a range of tasks which are directed towards a primary goal. The institution's structure is designed to turn these tasks into routines, and thus achieve the goal as efficiently as possible. Turning tasks into routines means defining roles for the people who are involved in the institution. Smooth operation of the institution requires that these people co-operate in adopting their assigned roles.

In a general hospital the tasks carried out relate to the care of sick people and treatment of disease. The goal of care and treatment is the cure of disease. Tasks are allotted according to roles, most of which are familiar to us as professional occupations; doctor, nurse, social worker, and so forth. Less well recognized, however, is the fact that patients and families are also allocated roles in the institution. Conformity to these roles enables the staff to perform their tasks smoothly and efficiently. Departures from the expected patient or family role can disrupt the pattern of care and upset the staff.

A particularly important feature of role allocation in an acute-care institution is the way in which the patients' physical needs are distinguished from social, emotional and spiritual aspects of need. People who are patients are expected to delegate responsibility for their physical needs to the hospital staff, but retain responsibility for their feelings and thoughts about the meaning of their illness. People who are in staff roles are expected, by the patients and by themselves, to be highly skilled in meeting physical needs, but staff have little or no expectation of being able to help in emotional or spiritual crises. Of course, there are some staff roles which are designed to help patients at the point of social, emotional or spiritual need, but in a general hospital these roles are secondary to those dealing with physical care and cure.

The policy of splitting physical need from other aspects of personal need becomes a problem when a general hospital attempts to provide terminal care. This is not to say that it is not a problem at other times – it certainly can be – but in most cases people with curable disease are prepared to accept the patient role with its compartmentalizing of their need because they expect to be cured and discharged in the not too distant future. Emotional problems and questions of meaning can be held over pending a return to normal life. Dying people, however, have no such expectation to balance the concessions required by the patient role. Their social, emotional and spiritual needs are acute, and they should not be expected to deal with them on their own. They need to be cared for as whole people.

Staff will be well aware of the range of a dying person's needs, but that awareness may make them feel uncomfortable. Even when concentrating on the physical care of a dying patient, staff may feel inadequate because they cannot meet those needs as they would like; that is, by bringing about a cure. Staff whose efforts are normally directed towards curing patients will often find it unsatisfying to provide palliative care alone, or even feel it an affront to their professional competence to be required to do so. Even where physical care is concerned, a dying person does not fit easily into the pattern of care of a general hospital. When in addition to being a symbol of failure of curative treatment the dying person seeks help with emotional or spiritual issues, staff discomfort can become acute.

The solution so far as many staff members are concerned is to avoid wherever possible potentially painful contact with the dying person. Some will simply stay away as much as they can, and control the nature and length of time they do spend with the dying person. Basic physical care must be maintained, but this will be handled as routine. Any more personal interaction will be avoided; staff withdraw emotionally from the person who is dying. This withdrawal can take place both with dying patients who are aware of their prognosis, and with dying patients who are unaware but who might ask questions or initiate conversations which could bring them into awareness.

Staff members' unavailability for any intimate personal contact with a dying person can be signalled in a variety of ways. Some of them become quite sophisticated strategies in a hospital, but even then most are still based on the sort of strategies any one of us might use to avoid close and potentially painful or unpleasant contact with another person. It is worth digressing slightly to look at some of the ways in which we can control the level of our involvement with dying people.

One of these is through what could be called non-verbal cues; the attitudes which we communicate with our bodies, irrespective of what we might be saying. This body language is expressed through personal style and touch and physical proximity, things which are very significant to hospitalized people. A bed-ridden patient may be touched numerous times each day in the most physically intimate ways, and yet be starved for the unsolicited touch which says 'I care for you.' Personal space is another factor. The world of a dying person who is close to the end often seems to be contracted to a small space about the pillow. To communicate properly we have to be within this space, sitting close, holding hands, listening and speaking at the person's pace. If we shy away from touching and avoid coming close to a dying person it doesn't matter what fine words we may say from the end of the bed; our behaviour will be giving the clear message, 'I really don't want to get involved with you.' Conversely, if we are prepared to communicate through physical nearness and touch this can speak more powerfully of care and concern than any mere words.

Another way we can signal our underlying attitudes or feelings is through our use of cheerfulness. Sometimes our sense of humour can be one of the most helpful gifts we can bring to another person, creating real intimacy between us. On other occasions, however, we can use cheerfulness as a defence, a way of saying, 'Let's keep this conversation light and breezy; I don't want to get serious here.' Cheerful behaviour is ambiguous, at least from another person's perspective. We need to be sensitive to the other person's feelings and in touch with our own underlying attitudes to decide whether our cheerfulness is appropriate or inappropriate to the situation.

The very way in which we offer help can also have self-protective or defensive elements about it. There is a tendency for most people who are helpers to go in for mothering at times; and it's a particular temptation for professional helpers such as nurses and chaplains. Like cheerfulness, a nurturing or mothering attitude can at times be very helpful and reassuring to a patient. But mothering can be very unhelpful if helpers get stuck in this state, making it their helping style, able only to relate to patients as a mother to a child. This is a particular danger for those caring for very sick or confused patients who cannot express themselves clearly. There is a tendency for helpers to interpret everything the patient says at a child's level; as requests for food, for reassurance or for physical attention. The possibility that the person, despite his communication difficulties, might be trying to relate at an adult level somehow is not considered. Because the helpers are locked into a mothering stance, and are not open to relate as adults with another adult, the patient's communication is devalued or discounted entirely.

A common way of avoiding a close relationship while still looking after another person is to concentrate on tasks which exclude listening to or talking with that person. Such tasks may be those involved in routine physical care; or during a visit we may set ourselves to talk so much that the patient cannot introduce the sort of agenda that might make us uncomfortable; even religious tasks such as prayer and reading scripture may be used to keep our distance from another person. While it is important to give care a practical expression, it is also possible to become obsessed with caring tasks in such a way that true care falls away, and the other person becomes an object around which we focus our activity, rather than a person with whom we share our life. In the final analysis, the most significant help we can offer to a dying person is our caring presence in a genuine relationship. It is who we are, more than what we do, that really counts.

In a hospital, avoidance strategies like this are often used to maintain a split between physical care and emotional and spiritual care. By adopting behaviour like that described above staff members can have access to patients' symptoms and can treat the physical signs of their disease without having to deal with the patients' feelings and questions about what their illness means for them as persons. Strategies which limit the openness of staff-patient relationships are most obvious in dealing with patients who suspect that they are terminally ill, and with those who know that they are terminally ill and are struggling to come to terms with that knowledge.

The most extensive documentation of staff-patient relationships in terminal care is probably that of Glaser and Strauss and their associates.[12] These researchers gathered their material through non-participant observation of terminal care in general hospitals, principally in the USA but supplemented with work in the United Kingdom, Europe and Asia. In the course of their study they discovered that behaviour associated with terminal illness can be described and analysed in terms of the way information is distributed among participants in the dying process. They proceeded to do this through what they termed 'awareness contexts'. The dying person's movement through these contexts, from the point of diagnosis to the point of death, they called a dying trajectory.

Glaser and Strauss' work is now somewhat dated, as it has made its contribution to reforming contemporary hospital practice. Nevertheless, it is worth outlining their findings in some detail. You may feel that things are different now; and in many hospitals policies concerning information offered to terminally-ill patients have in fact altered. But it is only in the last decade that changes have been initiated. We should not lose sight of the situation which required reform, for it is still with us in many institutions, even if the form of the problem has been modified somewhat. And while policies may have changed in some places, by and large the institutional structures and the training methods which supported the old policies remain.

In Glaser and Strauss' study, most dying trajectories began in closed awareness, the situation where the patient does not know that he has a terminal illness, but the staff and family usually do know and have elected not to inform the patient. Glaser and Strauss found that closed awareness was the state preferred by hospital staff, and that they endeavoured to maintain it for as long as possible.

Closed awareness is reinforced by a number of features of hospital organization which reflect the assumption that information is hospital property and will not be volunteered readily to the patient or his family. For example, medical records are secured in most institutions and are not made available to other than medically-trained personnel, while the person who is designated as the one to provide information is usually a senior consultant who is seldom available to patient or family. However, because most patients will insist on knowing something about their condition, the staff's desire to maintain closed awareness may produce a fictitious case history. This consists of information and actions designed to keep the patient hoping for recovery, and it is built up by telling only part of the truth, by evading direct questions, even by deliberate misinformation. Attempts may be made to divert a patient's attention from significant clues by prescribing further marginally-relevant tests, or even in extreme cases by initiating false treatment. Conversations which staff have with the patient are recovery-oriented, and carefully limited to the present or the immediate future. The risk of staff members inadvertently revealing clues to the real situation is reduced by spending less time with the patient, and filling that reduced time with routine tasks.

Usually the family is told of the patient's prognosis and recruited to join with the staff in keeping information from the patient. Sometimes, however, the family is also kept in ignorance, or just one 'strong' family member may be told and enlisted in a conspiracy to keep the news from the others. Many of the tactics employed in keeping the family unaware are the same as those used for the patient. Staff will avoid the family as much as possible, while those junior staff members who cannot avoid contact will be able to use the defence: 'I'm not allowed to say – you'll have to see Dr A, but he's not free at the moment.'

The reasons for preferring closed awareness are not always expressed explicitly. The most common reason given is that 'the patient's hope must not be taken away'. Associated with this is a fear that a patient who knows that he is dying may become deeply depressed, even suicidal. There is a risk too that he might become a management problem if he no longer sees himself as dependent on the staff to help him recover. Behind these proffered reasons, however, lie a number of unadmitted, perhaps unrecognized, factors personal to the staff, as indicated earlier.

Closed awareness is initiated by the doctor deciding to withhold information about a patient's diagnosis and prognosis. The burden of maintaining closed awareness, however, falls upon the nursing staff who have the most sustained contact with the patient. A similar burden falls on the aware family. Sooner or later closed awareness will break down, principally because the fictitious case history is being maintained by so many people that inconsistencies are bound to appear. This breakdown leads to suspicion awareness.

In suspicion awareness the patient or the unaware family are between complete ignorance and full awareness, and a contest for information commences. The patient attempts to confirm her suspicions; usually the staff try to keep her from full awareness. Suspicion awareness can be triggered in a number of ways. It may be brought about through inconsistencies in the information provided by the staff; it may be that the patient recognizes her symptoms as serious; it may be that the physician in charge deliberately gives hints of a grave prognosis in order to prepare the patient for the news that is to come. Sometimes the changed behaviour of family, staff or other patients is the clue which triggers suspicion awareness; even her location in the hospital may raise questions in the patient's mind. Suspicion may show itself openly, with the patient putting direct questions to anyone who might know something more; or she may keep her suspicions to herself, waiting for further information to confirm or deny them.

Family suspicions seldom lead to a prolonged contest for information. The doctor will usually take the opportunity to bring them into the picture and prepare them for the patient's death. In fact there are several institutional strategies designed to initiate suspicion which can be led on into full awareness. The critically-ill list is one common method of alerting relatives that death is a possible outcome. Another

way is the doctor announcing, 'There's nothing more we can do,' or
'It's out of our hands now.' The opening is given for the family to
draw their own conclusions and verify them with questions if they so
desire.

Suspicion awareness may at times include the nursing staff. A
doctor may choose to withhold information from them, hoping thereby
to maintain the quality of nursing care which the patient receives; for
a reduction in nursing attention given to terminal patients has been
quite widely reported. In some cases the patient's suspicions may be
encouraged or deliberately induced in the hope of bringing the patient
into full awareness. If this is the case, there is no contest for information
between patient and staff, and the transition from suspicion to full
awareness is swift. Staff who prefer dying patients to be fully aware
of their situation are, however, something of an exception. More
frequently staff respond to patient suspicions with a series of tactics
designed to reduce suspicion or eliminate it altogether and return the
situation to closed awareness.

If this latter situation is the case, a patient's suspicions are more
likely to be expressed in subtle ways than in direct questioning. He
may announce that he is dying, and watch for staff reactions; or he
may set conversational snares to elicit inconsistent information. He
may attempt to sneak a look at his records. Staff will respond by
intensifying and elaborating the methods used to maintain closed
awareness. They will close ranks, striving to eliminate inconsistencies
in the fictitious case history, evading the patient's probing, using their
authority to indicate directly or indirectly to the patient that he is
going too far and should be prepared to trust them rather than
continue to pressure them for further information.

Suspicion awareness is inherently unstable. It is fuelled by the
patient's anxiety, and it places considerable strain on the staff who
choose to counter the patient's anxious probing. It usually passes
quite rapidly to a state of full awareness. Nevertheless, because
suspicion awareness puts such pressure on the staff, it influences
hospital procedure in general: nearly all hospital work is organized in
such a way that a suspicious patient can be kept at arm's length, even
if there is no such patient in the ward at that particular time.

Glaser and Strauss distinguished two forms of full awareness. In
both forms everyone involved knows the prognosis, but only in open
awareness is this fact admitted publically and discussed among the
participants. The other form of full awareness is mutual pretence
where all participants, while knowing that the patient is dying, tacitly
agree to behave as if nothing is the matter. Mutual pretence is thus

an elaborate acting out of 'business as usual'. On the surface everything appears to be normal, the hospital routine continues smoothly, and the patient and staff appear to be on the best of terms. A careful observer might note that only safe, non-threatening topics are discussed, and that the patient particularly is very sensitive to the staff. In fact he is a model patient; polite, co-operative and appropriately grateful. The individual participants will have their own feelings about the true situation, but they will struggle with these and do their weeping on their own. Private anxiety or grief will not be allowed to enter into or disturb the tranquility of the public relationships. If the mask slips momentarily, and someone shows his underlying feelings, the others will usually ignore him until he regains his composure.

Mutual pretence usually comes about when the staff are clearly uneasy about discussing death with a patient. If a suspicious patient has had to confirm his suspicions in the face of staff discomfort and evasiveness, he may well keep silent once he knows his prognosis rather than risk alienating the staff any further. It may seem to him better to relate even at the superficial level of mutual pretence than risk a complete breakdown of personal relationships with death out in the open.

There are two major staff rationales for joining in pretence. Firstly that if the patient wishes to pretend it may be better for his health to do so and, secondly, that staff can give better care if the patient does not have to be faced openly. This may well be so; but it shows little awareness from the staff of their own role in setting up the conditions for mutual pretence. In marked contrast to this, staff will seldom enter into mutual pretence with the family. Rather, the family is expected to 'face facts', and a pretending family is likely to be confronted by the staff. However, family mutual pretence with the patient is acceptable.

There is far less strain on staff in mutual pretence than in suspicion awareness, for example. There can be some difficulties if a patient oscillates between mutual pretence and open awareness, wanting to talk about his imminent death one day, wishing to avoid the subject altogether on the next. For the patient, too, there are benefits in that mutual pretence at least provides some dignity and recognition compared with other awareness states in which he is being controlled by staff wishing to withhold information from him. However, mutual pretence denies the possibility of genuinely close relationships between patient and staff, and patient and family if the latter are also involved in the game.

Mutual pretence can move into open awareness in a number of ways. The transition may occur if the patient becomes so sick that reality breaks through pretence; but may well revert to pretence if the patient goes into remission. The transition may be selective; a dying person may choose to be open with one or two people while pretending with the rest. The movement from pretence to open awareness may be contested if some participants want to keep pretending. A patient moving quickly to the point of wanting to talk openly about his death may find family or staff opposing him for 'giving up'. Alternatively, if staff signal their awareness of approaching death by reducing active treatment, the patient and family may wish to 'keep on fighting' rather than move into open awareness.

Open awareness of course may come about without ever involving mutual pretence. This may be so particularly if the patient realizes that staff are open to talking about death and will not become evasive or defensive if she raises the subject. Yet even in open awareness, where direct communication is possible on most issues, tension can emerge. Much of it centres around acceptable behaviour; what it is to be a good patient, what is an appropriate way to die. This can be quite an acute problem if staff and patient belong to different social or cultural groups, and have little understanding of each others' background and values. While open awareness gives a dying person much more control over her dying, enabling her to order her personal affairs, make arrangements for her family, and say her farewells, she is still expected to be subject to the hospital's criteria for acceptable behaviour.

I have presented this outline of institutional strategies in fair detail because I believe that any attempts to improve the quality of care offered to dying people and their families requires an understanding of the social and institutional context of dying as well as an understanding of the processes individuals might go through. I have chosen to use Glaser and Strauss' framework to do this because I think that it is a useful analysis, readily recognizable to anyone who has been involved in a hospital structure in any capacity, and focussed around a central issue in terminal care, information control. Whether we have been patient, family member or professional helper, we have all experienced in some form the dilemma created by our assumption that while a patient owns a disease the doctor owns the diagnosis. We have all been involved in the strategies of information control described above.

I admit that the Glaser and Strauss analysis is a rather stark description of institutional care, and those of us who identify strongly with a helping profession may feel hardly done by.[13] I think it is true to say that the Glaser and Strauss method of non-participant observation has given them little sympathy or insight into what it feels like to care for terminally-ill patients. Nevertheless I would maintain that their analysis does uncover some basic dynamics of institutional care and that even if it is a little unsympathetic it is appropriate in so far as medical perspectives still tend to dictate terms in terminal care. Of course each of us knows of professional helpers who do not have to resort to the strategies described, who do not need to protect themselves from their patients, and who can open up and offer a helpful and healthy relationship to a dying person. But I would suggest that these exceptional people have been able to transcend the helping role taught to them in their training and given to them by their institution. They are people who add to their professional skills qualities of personal maturity and sensitivity, enabling them to respond first and foremost as fellow human beings to their dying patients. We need to find new ways to care for dying people, especially in our professional provision of care: we need to find ways of training professionals so that they can transcend the limitations of their institutional roles.

A basic conclusion to be drawn from this survey of institutional care is that the behaviour of most professional helpers with dying people is very similar to the behaviour of anyone else. To paraphrase Glaser and Strauss' conclusions, only the more technical behaviour of doctors and nurses in particular is professional; the rest is profoundly influenced by 'commonsense' assumptions which are essentially untouched by professional or even rational considerations or by current advances in psycho-social knowledge. The idea that staff are accountable for physical care but non-accountable for social or emotional aspects of care has resulted in physical care being less effective precisely because of the low priority given to these other aspects of care.

The description of institutional care also gives us further insight into the question raised in discussing the models of an individual's dying process: how does a dying person's environment affect the process? Which attitudes are encouraged and which suppressed in institutional care? We see here that institutional policy normally tries to stop people considering their own death. When and if patients discover or infer their prognosis staff and perhaps family often want the patient to return to denial or adopt an attitude of calm and hopeful acceptance of death. Other attitudes and feelings which, as we have seen, must be encountered in some form in moving from denial towards acceptance – anger, guilt, depression, bargaining – are all unacceptable to the institution. Sanctions are applied where they appear, particularly for angry or bargaining patients. Unfortunately the institution thus obstructs a patient's progress towards acceptance and realistic hope. In blocking apparently negative feelings the staff and family effectively ensure that a dying patient who cannot maintain denial is forced into depression and resignation: reference to the 'dramas of dying' table on page 3 will make this clear. The institution's implicit requirement that a patient be calm and cheerful is thus thoroughly counter-productive. This dilemma faces every institution which ignores or gives a low priority to social, emotional and spiritual aspects of care.

Communication in terminal illness

Maintaining adequate communication between medical personnel, patients and their families is a perennial problem in hospitals. It is a problem which often becomes acute in caring for dying people, as the preceding section shows. Difficulties emerge particularly because controls on the availability of information are built into the institution's caring routines. Changes in the way information is handled would thus have implications for the whole way in which institutional care is organized, and hence for the personal equilibrium of everyone involved in the institution. Changing the way information is handled ultimately means changing the nature of the personal relationships which exist within the institution.

I am emphasizing this link between communication and the nature and quality of personal relationships for several reasons. One of these is to challenge an assumption underlying much of the medical literature on communication in terminal illness. This literature usually details the defensive strategies a patient might adopt to shield himself from the threat of death, and gives advice to staff which assumes that they are free to adopt whatever attitude or stance is most helpful to the patient.[14] From our previous discussion this clearly is not the case. Such an approach ignores the fact that staff too are bound by their feelings and attitudes towards death, and that changing behaviour involves personal cost, just as there is cost for the dying person in working through the issues of dying.

A further reason for underlining the link between communication and relationships is to suggest that giving attention to the quality of personal relationships will lead to a corresponding improvement in the effectiveness of the physical care which is offered. Perhaps the clearest example of the interdependence of communication and physical care is in the area of pain control. Obviously a patient suffering severe pain will be unable to concentrate on anything else, and communication is blocked. Pain relief is required before communication can begin and any sort of personal relationship be established or renewed. There is, however, a clear association between physical pain and emotional stress, and the reduction of stress through an understanding, supportive relationship can contribute significantly to pain control. That is, attention given to communication enhances physical care. The startling increase in the quality of terminal care which can be achieved through a dual focus on good comfort care and open communication is demonstrated by the growing hospice movement.[15]

Yet another issue in communication is worth noting here. It is the difficulty of maintaining personal contact with confused patients. Confusion is a term used to describe a variety of conditions. It may be applied to a person whose behaviour is seen by others to be unrealistic, or it may indicate forgetfulness, speech difficulties, lack of orientation in time and place, erratic moods, or hallucinations. Such confusion has many possible causes. It is frequently reversible, brought on by a sudden traumatic incident like a fall or a surgical procedure, or even a mild respiratory infection in older people. Here confusion will usually pass once the person has adjusted to the sudden stress. But confusion may also be irreversible, and perhaps progressive, caused by a lesion in the brain. In terminal illness both forms of confusion are encountered quite often. Temporary reversible confusion may result from malnutrition or dehydration, infection, drug side-effects, and a variety of other causes. Irreversible confusion may arise from damage to the brain, often caused by secondary growths in the case of people dying with cancer.

It is not easy to communicate with someone who is in a confused state; and although episodes of confusion are experienced by a significant proportion of all hospitalized patients there is little or no literature available to help on this issue. In practice both family and professional helpers tend to concentrate solely on physical care, ignoring statements which are made by the confused person or responding in pacifying ways. In short, the confused dying patient is depersonalized. Particularly if he has suspected cerebral secondaries or some such irreversible brain damage, his statements and feelings may be regarded as little more than clinical indicators; they are not real, they are caused by the brain damage. Such an attitude, while clinically defensible, ignores the fact that the patient's perspectives and feelings are real to him. It is a specific example of a general tendency to which professional helpers are prone; we tend to view a patient's situation from our perspective, making judgments as to what is significant, what is peripheral, which needs should be met, which left aside. Sometimes we fail to realize that a patient's perspective can be very different. We may be worrying about his cancer; he may be worrying about something only tenuously related to this medical problem. If we ignore or belittle his concerns in order to devote our energies to what we see as the real problem, communication and trust between ourselves and the patient can start to break down. Good care at any level must take the patient's perspective into account.

Caring for dying people

In this chapter I have attempted to provide much of the background and context for the issues I will be dealing with in the remainder of the book. Already many of those issues will be clear from the way I have presented the material, but I would like to emphasize three guidelines which I believe need to be followed in any attempt to improve our care for the dying.

The first is that for care to be adequate it must be wholistic: that is, it must deal with the whole spectrum of the patient's need, for it is the whole person who faces death. This means that an adequate approach to care must be multi-disciplinary. Our present professional disciplines tend to fragment care, each concentrating on one particular aspect of a patient's need. Such an approach is counter-productive, and can lead to a dying person's experiences being discounted by a viewpoint which takes into consideration only some of his needs.

Secondly, any approach must take account of the whole system or network of relationships which is the context of dying. Otherwise we will find ourselves designing a model of care based only on the needs of the dying person in isolation, not seeing how families and institutions regulate behaviour while reinforcing certain attitudes and proscribing others. Or we may find ourselves recommending sweeping changes in institutional procedures and structures without realizing how those structures reflect people's emotional needs: institutional reform involves changes in the feelings and expectations of staff, family and patients. Finding new directions in caring for dying people will require a new understanding of helping relationships, which will in turn have significant implications for professional training and the organizing of professional care.

Thirdly and finally, a model of care cannot pretend to be value-free. It will inevitably contain implicit assumptions about issues like the meaning of suffering, what constitutes an appropriate death, what hope is. Assumptions like this need to be stated explicitly and grappled with in the light of our values and understanding of ultimate meanings. In this book, the particular framework used as a basis for values and meaning will be Christian theology.

2

· *Helping and Helplessness* ·

It is one thing to survey the literature and suggest some guidelines for constructing a model which gives a better understanding of terminal care. It is another thing entirely to develop a model general enough to explain the incredible diversity of human responses called forth by death, yet specific enough for practical caring strategies to be developed from it.

My own response in reflecting on this problem was to search for a unifying theme of some sort. I could see from the literature that many existing models for terminal care had too narrow a perspective. They focussed on an individual's psychological reactions, for example, and classified them while failing to deal with the context of those reactions – the person's family situation, the institutional procedures to which he was subject, and so forth. Other models took a sociological perspective, analysing the social processes in which a dying person was involved while failing to take account of the fact that essentially identical social contexts still produced a wide variety of individual response. A further shortcoming was that most models of care focussed on behaviour, describing patient behaviour and prescribing staff responses – if the patient does or says this, you must do or say that. Yet as we have seen already, words and actions can be highly ambiguous. The same words can be used by one person as an expression of despair and by another as a statement of hope. The same actions can be performed by one staff member to express concern, yet used by another to keep a dying person at an emotional distance.

Clearly we need to penetrate behind the ambiguous statements and activities, and find a perspective which integrates insights from a number of disciplines of study, if we are to develop an appropriate model for terminal care. The starting point for such a model must surely be in looking for the motivation behind the various responses to the dying situation, to ask what sort of human experience produces

these feelings and behaviours. One obvious answer of course is that
they are all responses to death. However, this does not take us much
further, largely because the sorts of behaviour and feelings we see and
experience in the face of death – our own or another's – are not unique
to death itself. They are common human responses, and so must
belong to a broader class of experiences. If we can find what that
is, analysing it should provide a basis for understanding human
behaviour in the face of death, and for developing a more appropriate
model of care.

As I continued to reflect on the question of finding a theme
underlying the diverse data of terminal care I gradually became
convinced that our responses to death are one example of our general
human responses to uncontrollable situations and the associated
feelings of helplessness. In this chapter I shall be developing this
proposition that the diverse behaviours seen in and around a person
who is dying are best understood as arising from helplessness. That
is, the source of such behaviour is denial, avoidance or acceptance of
the possibility or actuality of helplessness. How we actually feel and
behave of course varies, and depends among other things on our
personal development and our previous experiences with helplessness
and control.

I think that it is also important to say that this conviction that
helplessness could be an integrating theme arose out of reflection on
my own experience. In a chaplain's role particularly I had found
myself involved with dying people or their families in situations where
there was 'nothing more to do', in which we were all helpless. I had
found also that, paradoxically, if I was prepared to stay in these
situations, accepting my feelings of helplessness, then these were some
of the times I was most helpful as a pastor. However, the choice of
theme is not limited to my own experience. First person accounts by
relatives and professional helpers alike provide a considerable amount
of evidence that fear of helplessness or loss of control lies behind much
of the avoidance behaviour that is seen, and that the feeling of
helplessness arising from watching a loved person die and being
unable to do anything about it is probably the most painful part of
the relatives' experience.

Being helpless, which means being in a situation where the outcome
cannot be altered by any action we might take, usually leads to us
feeling helpless as well. In order to avoid these unpleasant feelings,
we may well try to avoid the situation itself; but if it cannot be avoided,
we must either deny or accept our feelings of helplessness. This latter
choice inevitably confronts a dying person, as physical helplessness is

unavoidable even if he or she focusses more on an inability to control some aspect of daily routine than on the underlying helplessness of living in a dying body. Relatives in contrast can avoid the situation, although complete avoidance seldom occurs as this would mean disowning the relationship. Some relatives, however, will stay away from the hospital altogether, or remain outside the patient's room rather than experience the helplessness of sitting by the death-bed. Other relatives are able to accept their helplessness and can begin to grieve constructively. Still others will want to deny their powerlessness, choosing to believe that somewhere a cure can be found, or that somehow a bargain can be struck with God who will allow the dying person to live.

The medical and paramedical staff, who usually have no prior relationship with the person now in their charge, have the broadest range of options open to them. Those most frequently chosen are forms of avoidance; avoiding the dying person or at least avoiding the subject of dying, using strategies like those outlined in the previous chapter. Doctors are the professionals with the most flexibility in ordering their work, and some will choose to absent themselves from a patient once there is 'nothing more to do', or avoid disclosing the actual situation by maintaining a largely-irrelevant treatment regime. The doctor's decreased attendance or apparent waning of interest is frequently a factor alerting patients to their terminal prognosis. A few doctors may even to all intents and purposes choose denial, fighting an aggressive medical rearguard action until after the patient has died, by which point it is the patient's fault for 'giving up while he still had a chance'. Responses like this either avoid encountering the limits of medical competence, or in effect deny that there are any such limits. A certain amount of the helplessness avoided by these methods is based on an unrealistic perception of terminal illness; for there is always more to do medically even when there is nothing more to do in the curative sense. But the contemporary emphasis on curative medicine is such that palliative care is often seen as having little value or interest or medical skill attached to it.

Avoidance is less easy for nurses, who must attend the patient throughout the working day, but nurses may choose to spend as little time as possible with a terminal patient, and when with the patient may concentrate solely on nursing tasks. This type of avoidance is reinforced by task-oriented training and by the way care is organized in most larger institutions. Chaplains may practice a similar avoidance by retreating behind liturgy rather than risking a personal encounter with a dying patient.[1] Each profession has its own variation on the theme of avoiding helplessness.

Descriptively, then, helplessness can be used as a theme to link together the disparate behaviours and feelings shown in the dying situation. If we are to develop some sort of model for understanding and organizing terminal care on this basis, we need first to look more systematically at the human experience of helplessness.

There are a variety of approaches which we could take at this point, for the ways in which we encounter and respond to helplessness are seen as basic to personality formation and development by a number of thinkers. Freud, for example, believed an infant's first painful experience of helplessness to be the content of anxiety; this original reaction to helplessness is then reproduced later in what are perceived as danger situations in the hope that the ego will be able to direct its course and avoid or master the danger. This danger signal, anxiety, is fundamental to the theory of repression and Freud's whole understanding of the structure of personality.[2] Philosophers of the existentialist school see a person's encounter with his ultimate helplessness in the face of finitude and death as being uniquely a situation which forces a decision as to whether he will live authentically and courageously in spite of his awareness of finitude, or inauthentically – avoiding or denying the encounters with helplessness which reveal the reality of our human situation.[3] Pursuing the theme of helplessness through these systems of thought is certainly instructive; but making a connection between the theoretical development and actual strategies for living is not easy because of the abstract framework used by many of these thinkers. Instead I have chosen to use here studies of helplessness performed by Martin Seligman and associates.[4] These studies, based on laboratory work with various animal species and with human subjects, provide a set of data which Seligman has extended to clinical problems of depression, aspects of child development, and sudden (voodoo) death. I will firstly outline the basic findings of his research, and then proceed to apply it to terminal care.

Learned helplessness

Seligman's experimental work proceeds from a simple definition of helplessness: a subject, human or animal, is helpless with respect to some outcome when that outcome occurs independent of all the subject's voluntary responses. Being helpless means being in a situation which is uncontrollable; and such situations can of course be set up easily in the laboratory. In addition to this objective sense of helplessness Seligman also uses the term to describe the subjective (psychological) state which typically results from experiencing uncontrollability. That is, he distinguishes the conditions of being helpless and feeling helpless.

Experimental studies show in general three types of disrupted behaviour associated with laboratory-induced or learned helplessness. Subjects show a reduced motivation to respond; their ability to learn is disrupted; and their emotionality is heightened. This three-fold disruption – motivational, cognitive and emotional – typifies helpless behaviour.

The experimental observation basic to Seligman's theory is that the situation of being helpless and the state of feeling helpless do not necessarily correspond. They usually do: but some subjects are rendered helpless even though objectively they have control of their situation, while others who are objectively helpless will continue to act as if in control. This implies an intermediate stage between the information a subject receives about his situation and the behaviour which results. Seligman represents this as follows:[5]

| Information about situation | → | Cognitive representation of the situation (learning, expectation, perception, belief) | → | Behaviour |

Thus it is the subject's expectation which determines the behaviour, not the actual situation in itself.[6] The expectation is related to the situation, but it also takes prior experience into account. If we expect on the basis of prior experience to be helpless in a particular situation (such as a maths test or a medical emergency at home), we probably will feel helpless, irrespective of the objective nature of that situation. Conversely, if we expect on the basis of prior experience to be in control of a certain situation we will probably not feel helpless even if objectively we are unable to affect the outcome. These general findings apply to human volunteers and also to a variety of animal species. In the case of animal subjects expectation of helplessness or control has to be formed by conditioning. For human subjects, however, this expectation may be formed merely by the experimenter telling a person that his situation is controllable or uncontrollable. Such an instruction will produce behaviour appropriate to the expectation irrespective of the actual objective situation – always providing that the subject is prepared to accept the experimenter's statement as true.

To this point we have been looking at results obtained under laboratory conditions where the only possible variable in an individual's evironment is under the experimenter's control. The crucial question for wider application of Seligman's theory is how these experimental observations relate to real-life situations, where each of us experiences a large number of variable factors, only some of which are controllable. Obviously in ordinary life we are subjected daily to uncontrollable experiences, whether it be riding on public transport or dealing with the vagaries of the weather. Equally obviously, very few of us are rendered helpless by such experiences. Seligman suggests that there are three major factors which influence our perception of uncontrollable situations in our lives so that only some lead to helpless behaviour. These factors are our past experiences with helplessness and control; our ability to accept a certain amount of helplessness in some areas of life provided that we have control of other areas; and the personal significance of the areas which are uncontrollable.

In practice these three factors seem to be inter-related and are perhaps better described as different aspects of our past experience and perception. The first factor arises from the observation that if we are used to being in control of our immediate situation we will tend to expect the outcome of any situation to be similarly controllable, and will act accordingly, it being difficult to convince us that an uncontrollable situation actually is uncontrollable. The converse is also true. A personal history of uncontrollability will make it difficult for us to believe that we can control any of the new situations in which we find ourselves. The second factor is that each of us has an ability to accept some situations in which we are helpless alongside situations over which we have control, without helplessness in one area affecting our performance in another. Again, this ability to discriminate between controllable and uncontrollable situations and to live in some sort of equilibrium between them without behaving helplessly, is related to our past experience and needs. Seligman's third factor, the relative importance to us of the uncontrollable areas of our lives, is again a function of our personal needs and personal history. All of us have some areas of life over which we need control. Even though we may tolerate uncontrollability in less important areas without being rendered helpless, uncontrollability in the important areas will lead to helpless behaviour, and this helplessness will generalize readily to less important areas; we will become immobilized.

What constitutes 'importance' in this sense is not very clear from Seligman's work. Related studies, however, indicate that important areas are ones which affect our feelings of personal competence. For example, in one study of problem-solving by depressed and non-depressed students it was found that when depressed students were able to attribute their failure to the difficulty of the problems rather than their own incompetence, their performance in problem-solving improved markedly.[7] The implication of this and similar studies is that failure in itself is not sufficient to produce helplessness; but failure which leads to a reduced sense of personal competence can render a person helpless.

More light is shed on Seligman's observations at this point by a related field of social learning theory which investigates control through positive reinforcement of subjects' controlling responses.[8] This approach, known as locus of control studies, is the converse of Seligman's method which looks at uncontrollability by breaking down controlling responses. Nevertheless, where they overlap the results of the two approaches are essentially in agreement, certainly in so far as the role of perception in helplessness and control is concerned.

Because Seligman's data come from a sharply-defined experimental context, his theory makes an absolute distinction between helpless and controlling subjects. This distinction is softened by locus of control studies which demonstrate that people can be categorized broadly in terms of their control needs as 'internals' or 'externals'. Internals are people whose control is internally-oriented – they rely mostly on information and understanding to be in control of their environment. Externals are people whose control is externally-oriented – they rely more on activity and social relationships for control. The differences between the two orientations are differences of degree. Externals tend to be helped by social stimulus during tasks, while internals are distracted or hindered by this. Externals are generally more socially responsive, while internals tend to resist social influence. Internals seem to be more cognitively alert than externals, and are more inclined to look for ways of understanding and controlling puzzling and uncertain situations. The groups also differ in the way they react to failure: externals tend to blame the circumstances, even when it is hard to justify this logically, while internals appear more objective in accepting failure or attributing blame. (Of course this latter judgment is being made by the experimenter, who presumably is an internal.)

The data concerning reaction to failure bring locus of control studies close to Seligman's investigations. Studies correlating mood with locus of control have shown that externals are more liable to depression in aversive circumstances, whereas internals tend to remain active in confronting what they apparently see as a challenge. These studies also noted that external locus of control is associated with a predominance of previous negative experiences with control.[9] Thus externals seem to correspond broadly with Seligman's category of subjects who incline towards helplessness in uncertain situations, while internals who gain their sense of control from personal resources or cognitive competence are more able to resist feeling helpless in such situations. Both helplessness theory and locus of control research are based initially on experimental animal studies. Experimental verification has not kept pace with the rate at which both theories have been extrapolated to consider human development and social problems in general. Isolated studies have checked some aspects of these extrapolations; of particular note is Seligman's work showing the marked similarity between laboratory-induced helplessness and clinical depression. He has used this apparent equivalence of helplessness and depression to develop a theory and therapy for depression.[10] As yet, however, these theories can claim rigorous verification only in the limited context of laboratory experiments. In their application to wider personal and social issues they are essentially descriptive.

It is in this descriptive way that I wish to use helplessness and locus of control theory. In the remainder of this chapter I want to employ some of the concepts outlined above in developing a model for relationships in terminal care. I will be raising a number of questions about current institutional practice, particularly current conceptions of the helping role, and suggesting alternative understandings.

Helplessness and control in terminal care

In applying helplessness theory to terminal care the temptation will be to introduce paragraph after paragraph with phrases like, 'as we have already seen', or 'in the previous chapter we noted that'. I will resist this temptation, pointing out at this stage that the assertions made here concerning terminal care may be substantiated from the literature reviewed in the first chapter.

The two key concepts from the preceding theory which I wish to apply to an understanding of behaviour in terminal care are these:

1. The desire to control our immediate circumstances, or at least avoid being rendered helpless by them, is a fundamental feature of human motivation.

2. Our identification of a situation as uncontrollable, resulting in helpless behaviour, depends upon our previous experience with uncontrollability, particularly as an infant. Because our perception is a function of our personal development, some of us can be rendered helpless by situations which could be controlled in some way, while others of us will continue to act as if in control of situations in which we are objectively helpless. An important related factor is that some of us, while believing ourselves to be helpless in a given situation, will

nevertheless be able to avoid feeling helpless if we see another
(benevolent) person to be in control of our situation.

The second of these concepts has of course been developed in detail
above. The first has only been touched upon, and an attempt to
substantiate it in detail would open up an enormous area of debate.
Nevertheless it could be pointed out that a desire for control has been
postulated as a central feature of human motivation in a number of
theories. One example at the instinctual level is Ardrey's hypothesis
of territorial imperative, an argument that man has not only retained
the territorial instincts of the animal kingdom but also the predator
instincts which can lead him to kill even members of his own species
in order to retain control of or extend his own territory.[11] From a
general psychological perspective R. W. White has argued that a
major part of human motivation can be described as a drive towards
competence, where competence is understood to include biological
viability as well as an ability to manipulate the environment. He
examines data from a whole range of psychological approaches,
from animal studies through to psychoanalytical ego psychology,
concluding that competent behaviour, producing a feeling of efficacy,
is a fundamental human need. We are not merely acted upon by our
environment, but we interact with it to establish order and control.[12]
Similar concepts underlie most philosophical understandings (and
most philosophical and scientific endeavour for that matter!).

Involvement in dying, whether as patient, relative or helper, will
inevitably confront us with limits to our competence. We will find
ourselves in situations in which there is nothing more to do; in which
the ultimate outcome cannot be affected by any of our responses, and
we are objectively helpless. But the point at which such a situation
arises, and our behaviour in that situation, depends upon our history
– how much control we need and what it is we need to control – and
on our environment – how much control we can retain.

Problems arise in institutional care when the control needs of
patient, family and staff are in conflict. This frequently is the case, for
a modern hospital is a particularly impoverished environment so far
as the control needs of a dying person are concerned. The difficulties
arise around the organization of care. Such a hospital requires patient
and family to commit control of care to the staff; in other words to
perceive the staff as being in control of a situation in which patient
and family are helpless. If patient and family are able to share this
perception and trust the staff to use their power benevolently, then
there will be no problem as long as this perception lasts; the patient
and family will avoid feeling helpless. If, however, they cannot share

the perception of medical control of the illness or bring themselves to trust the staff implicitly, conflict arises. The patient in particular finds himself dependent on people who will block his attempts to control his situation. He will be denied access to information which is basic to understanding and controlling his situation,[13] and his care and treatment will be programmed to suit the requirements of the staff, not according to his own needs. We have seen that patients with an internal locus of control need accurate information and understanding to control their situation, while for externals control of their environment and relationships is usually more important than information. By assuming control of both the immediate environment and access to information the institution contributes significantly to rendering both groups helpless. It is therefore not surprising that a large proportion of institutionalized patients exhibit helpless behaviour – depression and resignation. Remembering that the structure of institutional care is determined by the control needs of staff, we see that what is happening is that staff members, in an attempt to avoid their own helplessness, actually render patients helpless. Institutional structures amplify the helplessness which often accompanies illness.

To state the dilemma of institutional care in this way, however, does not imply that a better solution will be found by reversing the situation. Little or nothing is gained by an uncritical support of patient rights over and against the staff. One does not have to spend long in a hospital before meeting patients who, if given the control they want, could immobilize the entire institution! Rather, an examination of control and its effects leads us to recognize that the problem is one of sharing control, structuring institutional care so that the control needs of patient, family and staff can be met as far as possible. Clearly this will involve compromise: but not just the sort of compromise which characterizes contemporary medical care, where any conflict over control needs tends to be resolved in favour of the staff, who are permitted to assume power over patients.

If we want to care for dying patients in such a way that they live until they die, the implication is clear. Control must be shared in a way that allows patient, family and staff to remain as competent and in control as possible. Some details of institutional care then must become a matter for negotiation between the various parties. Each person needs to be able to share his perception of what is important for him to control so that arrangements for care can be made taking due consideration of these needs. In acute illness this is not too much of a problem, at least not initially. Almost without exception everyone involved has the goal of cure, and the patient and family willingly give to the staff the control which is claimed as necessary to make a cure possible. A temporary surrender of personal rights is acceptable in view of the longer term goal of renewed health. It is in terminal care, at the point of nothing more to do, that needs come into conflict and negotiation will become significant. The goal of care now becomes comfort, not cure; and to co-operate in making a person comfortable the staff must bring about a quite radical change in their attitudes from overcoming disease within a patient to attending to the personal needs of that patient. This change from a focus on symptoms to a focus on the person is not easily made,[14] and can lead to conflict in which the patient's needs are minimized or virtually ignored in order to maintain the staff's defences.

The change of focus may also require staff to set aside their clinical perspective in order to understand and evaluate events from the patient's point of view. For example, it is not uncommon for terminally-ill people to be more concerned about their bowels than the primary medical problem, their cancer. From a clinical perspective constipation is a secondary outcome, trivial in comparison with the cancer. From the patient's perspective, however, it may be central, and if the staff cannot appreciate this and respond to the patient's concern it can be the beginning of a breakdown in staff relationships with the patient: he will feel that the staff simply are not taking him seriously. Dealing with constipation may seem a minor matter to a clinician, but for many patients it is a crucial control issue. Whether it is a function of a particular generation's toilet training I do not know; but there seem to be a number of older people who can cope with almost anything provided their bowels operate regularly, but become depressed and introspective if they don't.

It would of course be naive to assert that control can always be shared in such a way that everyone will be able to feel competent. Difficulties arise in terminal care, particularly with patients whose control needs simply are not compatible with their physical or mental state. A person whose control needs are met through physical activity feels helpless when his body is rendered helpless. If a sense of competence is to be regained this person needs to find other means of personal fulfilment. LeShan's programme of personal growth for dying patients is an example of one relatively successful attempt at meeting such a need.[15] In encouraging terminal patients to wish and imagine, explore their feelings about life and discuss their strengths, actual and potential, LeShan found that some sort of understanding and acceptance of death appeared as a by-product of his work. Of course less resolvable situations frequently occur in terminal illness.

Many patients will not have the time, opportunity or personal resources to change in this way. Others whose control needs are met through their mental abilities may be rendered helpless if these faculties are disrupted by a stroke or an episode of confusion. Others again may retain their mental capacities but be unable to perceive any meaning or hope in their circumstances. Sometimes there is no way for feelings of helplessness to be avoided.

For the staff, not taking all control from the patient means accepting limitations. These will include admitting explicitly the actual limits to medical competence rather than acting as if medical science is omnipotent and any failure the patient's fault. Even this degree of realism can be painful for some staff members who would prefer not to make such admissions. In some cases the decision to share control with a patient will mean acting contrary to staff preferences regarding information control or ward organization. For example, a staff member who feels more comfortable working in open awareness with dying patients nevertheless should not force awareness on a patient who prefers not to know the details of her situation. Neither should a frail or unco-ordinated patient who gains an important sense of control from feeding herself be denied this opportunity, even if it does take a long time and means more cleaning up afterwards.

So far the discussion has centred around control of information and behaviour. Behind these matters is the further issue of reaching an understanding or finding a meaning in the situation. Even if access to information and ward routine can be negotiated in such a way that a dying person can operate competently at an everyday level, she will still face helplessness if ultimately she cannot find meaning in her life. The person who can find or re-affirm meaning will be in control of her situation, able to understand and accept her death. The person who can find no meaning will be helpless: depressed, resigned, hopeless.

The actual meaning discovered or reaffirmed will vary from person to person. One person may believe that despite his own (objective) helplessness God is in control of the situation and so he need not feel helpless. Another may share the same perception but feel herself under judgment, awaiting death in stoic resignation and despair. Yet another will anticipate death as the end of his existence, placing his hopes in the continuing success of the children he leaves behind. That each person reaches the point of perceiving and affirming a meaning for his or her life is a fundamental goal of pastoral care. Such a meaning cannot be delivered to a dying person; but the other people involved with him can certainly help or hinder him in finding his own meaning. The perpetuation of conflict over control of information and organization of care is a major factor which impedes people in institutional care from discovering meaning and accepting their deaths. Resolving that conflict in such a way that dying people can confront questions about meaning within a caring supportive relationship is a major responsibility of good care.

This claim of course returns us to the point made towards the end of the previous chapter, that different aspects of care cannot be divorced from one another and tackled in isolation. Even if the task of finding meaning in dying is essentially a pastoral responsibility, for example, it still requires that conflict around medical aspects of care be resolved adequately. Conversely, the adequate performance of medical care cannot stop short of confronting questions of meaning. The sort of care involved in negotiating and sharing control among patients and staff is open ended: it recognizes that we help to meet each others' needs, that within a helping relationship we help each other, and that there are no narrow limits to be set on a relationship like this. If I am to help you as a doctor, a nurse, or a chaplain, I must be prepared to share with you not only my technical expertise but also what I have discovered as a human being about living in a world like this.

If we are to care for dying people in different and better ways it is our understanding of the helping role that must change. Without this, changes in institutional structure or organization of care will be of little use. Helpers must change, and in turn revise the structures which accommodate and express their caring. It is to a consideration of the helping task and how it must change in the light of the previous discussion that we now turn.

The helping role

Any contemporary understanding of the helping role is strongly influenced by the doctor-patient relationship. Paramedical professions use this model in institutional work, in part because in a hospital these professions operate under medical direction. Even the non-institutional practice of professions like social work and counselling still borrow heavily from it.

The doctor-patient relationship in fact represents, in a focussed form, the characteristics of most relationships within the institution. As head of the medical and paramedical team which cares for the patient, the doctor makes many decisions which he does not have to implement, exerting control over those below him in the institutional hierarchy as well as the patient. Nurses in particular feel the tension of this, aware of patients' personal needs which may conflict with treatment but perceiving themselves as bound by doctors' orders. Nevertheless they will usually identify themselves with those orders, presenting a united front to patient and family. In general the staff publically adopt the doctors' position, particularly in the event of conflict. Even the patient's family tends to be allocated to one side or the other in doctor-patient contests. They may be treated in the same way as the patient, denied access to information and controlled by the staff in their time and behaviour with the patient; or they may be enlisted as allies of the staff, helping to control the patient's behaviour or the information available to him.

A fundamental feature of the professional helping relationship is the establishing and maintaining of a competence gap between the expert professional and the lay patient or client. Obviously such a gap does exist in the area of professional expertise – knowledge of disease processes or of the social welfare system, for example. But there is a tendency for these professional relationships to be very deliberately contained to the area of the professional's competence. The professional thus presents as an expert in all aspects of the relationship, and the effect of this is that the competence gap becomes absolute, the professional seeming to be more competent and more authoritative in all areas of life.

The doctor-patient relationship then is not a normal open-ended human relationship, but one which is carefully defined and which has associated with it a number of undeclared assumptions about each person's part in the relationship. The covert nature of these assumptions heightens the possibility that each will have unrealistic expectations of the other, and indeed this frequently occurs in practice. Patients will come to a doctor with messianic expectations of his knowledge and skill, his power to save and deliver. He is expected both to know the solution to a problem and to take physical action to solve it. To express uncertainty or reservation instead of an authoritative diagnosis, to give mere advice instead of a prescription, will often be regarded by a patient as a failure in medical competence rather than an accurate assessment of the situation and the patient's needs (as contrasted with his wants). On the other hand, doctors' expectations of patients may be similarly unrealistic. Some doctors expect patients to assess their symptoms with sufficient accuracy to know which are significant and when they should present themselves to a doctor; and then they expect them to defer totally to the doctors' assessment once he has been consulted. The patient's decision to consult the doctor becomes in effect a decision to relinquish responsibility for his health.

With unrealistic expectations like this on both sides, there is plenty of potential for conflict in the doctor-patient relationship. The more authoritative the doctor's stance, the more likely it is that there will be conflict with patients who wish to be involved in the assessment and treatment of their illness.[16] Frequently the conflict will not be acknowledged within the relationship; the patient will quietly ignore or modify medical advice without making an issue of it. At other times the conflict will surface, with the patient demanding another opinion or using open non-compliance in an attempt to get the doctor to change treatment.[17] Again, this conflict seems to have its source in differing perspectives and differing control needs. For the doctor, illness is his work; for the patient, it is a disabling of himself. The doctor's assumption of control over his work is incompatible with the patient's need for independence. In an institution this conflict is intensified because the institution exists to manage and carry out medical work.

The degree of conflict in the doctor-patient relationship seems to be a function both of the patients' need for independence and the doctor's view of his professional role. An implication of this is that there is no one ideal stance for a doctor to adopt. An authoritative stance may lead to severe conflict with one patient, but be most acceptable and reassuring to another. A more open and permissive stance may help one, but disappoint another. The ideal presumably is a doctor who is able to assess his patients' needs and respond appropriately while leaving the way open to help that patient move towards taking greater responsibility for his own health care. However, such flexibility assumes considerable self-understanding on the part of the doctor.

Doctors who relate to patients in stereotyped ways and limit disclosure as much as possible tend to be those who emphasize the exclusiveness of professional status and the competence gap between themselves and their patients. In order to preserve their autonomy they feel the need to keep tight control of consultations. In contrast, doctors with more flexible attitudes to communication place less emphasis on status and the competence gap, and the doctor-patient relationship is more egalitarian and reciprocal.[18] Conflict is then most acute with a doctor who sees his competence being brought into question when a patient is not willing to surrender control to him. Such a conflict is more than a physician's work versus patients' independence issue: rather, the doctor appears to perceive a threat to competence as a threat to his personal identity.

I think that here we have an important clue to understanding why failure in a medical task, even failure to cure a dying patient, can be so acutely painful for some doctors. I would suggest that these doctors, through their training with its emphasis on curative scientific medicine and the sheer volume of work which precludes non-medical interests, have invested their self-understanding and identity in their professional role. Such a person does not see himself as Tom Jones who happens to work as a doctor, but Tom Jones the Doctor. Anything perceived as a threat to medical competence becomes a threat to personal identity, and the possibility of medical impotence – nothing more to do – can make him feel utterly helpless. This stands in contrast to the professional whose identity is not centred in his professional role. Situations may make him helpless relative to his professional skills, unable to do anything to alter the outcome, but he is less likely to feel helpless because his personal competence is not under threat in the same way.

Such a confusion of personal and professional identity is of course by no means peculiar to doctors. It seems to be present to a greater or lesser degree in all professions. To take another example: the ministry has a significant proportion of people unable to enter into open relationships with parishioners. Ministers who feel that they must have answers on every aspect of religious belief or human doubt, who cannot admit to any failing in their kindness or patience, or any negative emotion or attitude, will not be able to share openly with others, and will exert the same sort of control on pastoral relationships as the authoritarian doctor does with his patients. Each professional seems to live uneasily with the tension between an internalized ideal and his actual performance, and this may well be the reason behind the above-average need for control of relationships which is a general characteristic of helping personalities.[19]

When a helping stance like this is brought into institutional care the result is an attitude which allows staff to assume power over patients. Care is seen as a one-way transaction, delivered by strong, healthy staff to weak, sick patients. This paternalism is shown in communication, for a significant proportion of staff-patient communication has a parent-to-child character. The ambiguity of such attitudes has already been discussed. Certainly there are times when some parental nurturing is needed, but all too often the parent-to-child communication reinforces and increases the regression which accompanies illness. Such communication strategies are only one aspect of an underlying paternalistic attitude to care, further illustrated by the strict disciplinary regime of some wards, and practices like junior staff assuming the right to call elderly patients by their given names. These practices, tending to recall a patient's childhood, reinforce staff control and add to the patient's dependency.

The picture I have drawn so far is of a helping relationship established around particular professional tasks, controlled or limited by the helper to the area of professional competence. Even in professions which are not task-oriented in the same way, in which the helper-client relationship itself is the therapeutic tool, similar limits or controls appear. The therapist-client relationship is not understood as mutual. The patient is expected to disclose his feelings and attitudes as fully as possible, while the therapist is less personally involved.[20] A good example of this stance is Eissler's discussion of the psychiatrist's role with dying patients.[21] The psychiatrist must identify with the patient in some ways, Eissler believes, if he is in any sense to accompany the patient on his last journey. However, this partial identification 'must not lead to the evolvement (*sic*) of anxiety in the therapist. . . If the therapist's own fear of death is considerable, he will either recoil from even a partial identification, or become anxious, if not depressed. In both instances he is bound to harm the patient.'[22]

While accepting that as a professional helper (and as a human being) one cannot form deep relationships with everyone, I still believe that Eissler's view is a rationalization. The insistence that the professional helper should always be 'strong' is one of the most unhelpful aspects of this helping role. When this view is held, the helper inevitably begins to exert self-protective control on the relationship, particularly at points where the patient feels helpless, thus intensifying that person's helplessness.

This doctor-patient model of the helping relationship reinforces the power of the professional helper and makes it unlikely that control will be shared within the relationship. The scope of the relationship and the initiatives taken within it will be controlled predominantly by the professional. While this way of operating may be adequate to deal with many sorts of physical problems, it is not adequate to help a person who is dying. There are, however, other models for helping relationships, even if the doctor-patient model continues to dominate institutional care in particular and much social care in general.

An alternative understanding of the helping role is put forward by psychiatrists such as Carl Jung and D. W. Winnicott.[23] Here the helper-client relationship is seen essentially as a relationship between equals, with therapist and client together exploring the situation which is troubling the client, in the process each deriving personal benefit from their relationship. It is necessary to expand a little on what is meant by 'equal' here. Clearly it does not mean that therapist and client have identical functions in the relationship. Rather. equality is meant to underline their shared humanity – it is moral and spiritual equality. The professional is not necessarily a better human being because of his training. Another term used to recognize this fundamental equality as human beings is 'mutuality', or even more precisely 'asymmetric mutuality'. This indicates both the differing roles of therapist and client – other examples of asymmetric mutuality are mother and child or teacher and student – and the fact that the goal of the relationship is mutual growth or transformation. What happens in the therapeutic relationship will change the therapist as well as the client. Jung suggests in fact that if the therapist is not affected by what is happening nothing significant will come out of the relationship. In this sort of helping relationship then there is negotiation and sharing of control. Sometimes a therapist will need to assert his perspective over against the client; sometimes the client will need to do the same in withstanding the therapist's interpretations or suggestions or in initiating new directions in therapy.

More recently Sidney Jourard has taken this aspect of the mutual relationship between therapist and client even further.[24] He maintains that, if a helping relationship is to be of actual help, it is necessary for the helper to disclose himself within the relationship. That is, the helping relationship is to be open and mutual, affecting both participants, rather than a series of interpersonal transactions based on the assumption of a competence gap between helper and patient. What the patient needs is a relationship in which he can grow. The helper is to be a model, a person who is prepared and able to show what a free adult is like in the hope that this will help the other who is still hidden behind defences. A helping relationship helps by the helper making himself vulnerable – running the risk not just of professional inadequacy but of personal helplessness in order that change may come about. If the helper is not open to change, neither will the patient be open. Change within a relationship cannot be controlled by one of the participants – it can happen only through mutual commitment to the relationship.[25]

Clearly this understanding of a helping relationship is far more consistent with the implications of helplessness theory than is the more prevalent doctor-patient model. It indicates too that a body of theory and helping strategies is already available to draw upon in the practical application of helplessness theory. However this literature also emphasizes what is required of the helper: a commitment to continuing personal development, a capacity to reflect upon each relationship in which he or she is involved, and a willingness to forgo formal or stereotyped modes of helping behaviour.

Understood in this way, the helping relationship meets needs and poses threats for both participants. There is the possibility of intimacy and the possibility of helplessness. Both participants may change; but neither can control those changes. Professional helpers thus require personal integrity and maturity as well as professional skills – who they are matters as well as what they do – so that personal qualities and personal growth cannot arbitrarily be separated from professional practice. This clearly has implications for the training and continuing practice of helping professionals, and we will consider these further in chapter 7.

A change in the self-understanding of the helpers would imply corresponding changes in institutional practice, reflecting in the organization of care the mutuality of staff-patient relationships. Some institutional forms like this already exist within certain disciplines. In psychiatry, for example, the therapeutic community attempts to involve all its members, staff and patients alike, in working together to build a communal life. Role distinctions are minimized, and staff and patients support each other in working together at relationship problems. Staff need to acknowledge openly the patients' capacity to help not only each other but staff members also. Other variations on this form of social therapy exist, and it has had quite a wide influence in hospital psychiatric treatment in general.[26] The idea of a staff team approach has spread from psychiatric to general medical practice, but seldom are patients involved directly in determining their own treatment.

In terminal care such egalitarian methods are less likely to be feasible in view of the differing physical competence of patients and staff. However, this competence gap need not, and should not, be extended to emotional, social and spiritual aspects of life. Again, institutional forms exist which provide terminal care centring on patients' needs and in which the staff members' expert roles do not mean that they keep an emotional distance from their patients. Probably the best known form is seen in the hospice movement, and we will be considering this in some detail in chapter 6.

In conclusion, what can be said about the relevance of helplessness theory to terminal care? Firstly it does integrate the data, giving a framework for describing and understanding much of the disparate behaviour and attitudes which surround dying. Secondly and importantly, it gives some insight into ways of restructuring terminal care so that dying people are given the opportunity to live until they die. The model we have developed here shows both what needs to be done in restructuring institutional care to avoid at least some of the depression and resignation which characterize the lives of many people dying in institutional care. It also shows the links between these changes in the structure and method of care, the ways in which professional helpers do their caring, and the way these helpers understand themselves. In this sense we are moving towards a general model of care, not one limited simply to the dying situation. Central to this revised model of care is the recognition that relationships need to be mutual. Both partners in a relationship can support and learn from each other. Even in cases where the helper supports a helpless dying patient he is gaining from that experience knowledge which will help him in future caring relationships and in his own living and dying.

Achieving mutuality in relationships requires that the helper accept the risk of helplessness as well as the challenge of change. The only way in which the risk of helplessness can be avoided is so to control the relationship from the outset that it can never become mutual. If a helper maintains control at all costs, the medical model of care – or any other system in whose name he assumes power – becomes an idol: the system and its servants are seen in effect to be omnipotent.

The helplessness which is encountered in helping relationships may be objective or subjective. Objective helplessness is the situation where nothing more can be done to achieve a hoped-for outcome. When this situation is shared by patient and helper, and the helper is not made subjectively helpless through loss of his objective control of that situation, then the patient can also hope to retain control by discovering inner resources like those which sustain the helper. But sometimes his commitment to the other person can lead the helper into situations where he too will feel helpless. The helper then has the choice of abandoning the relationship and withdrawing, or staying and sharing the other person's helplessness. When this point has been reached any further professional action a helper might pursue is at best irrelevant. The choice is whether or not to remain involved; and the decision made depends on the personal maturity of the helper – who he is – rather than on his professional skills – what he can do.

The situations which present choices like this are on the boundary of the helping role, and although they are potentially present in every mutual relationship they will not occur in many ordinary caring encounters. In terminal care, however, they are not uncommon, as both helper and patient must at some point confront their helplessness in the face of death. This helplessness shared in mutual commitment need not be merely an aversive experience. Meaning and hope can grow out of it. It can lead to an experience of grace in which a person is transformed, where meaning emerges out of confusion and hope appears out of despair. Yet this grace cannot be guaranteed; it comes as a gift into the relationship, not as the inevitable outcome of the helper's relinquishing of control. Each time the helper chooses to share another person's helplessness he risks feeling abandoned himself, even though his hope will be that grace will appear through shared suffering.

The times in which a helper opens himself to another person and finds himself able only to share that person's helplessness are difficult and painful. They are also opportunities for the helper to grow. Frequently our feelings of helplessness arise from inappropriate self-expectations; we believe that there must be something we can do to change the situation, that because hope has not appeared in the person's life it must be a failure in our technique rather than, say, the result of that person's lifetime experience of hopelessness. Much of what affects a helping relationship most profoundly is beyond our responsibility; but it can take us a long time to realize and accept this. Encountering our own helplessness is a necessary part of discovering the limits to our skills and influence and seeing ourselves in a more realistic way.

In chapter 4 I will trace the process by which meaning and hope can come into a dying person's experience, and look at ways in which a helper can assist this process. Before doing this I want first to outline the values underlying the approach to care I am taking in this book. Thus in this next chapter we turn to a discussion of pastoral care and its relationship with the helping model put forward here.

3
· *Pastoral Perspectives* ·

In making a critique of contemporary practices in terminal care I have been viewing the situation from a pastoral perspective. The critique and the developments of the helplessness theme have not used theological language, and should stand alone as a person-centred critique of terminal care. But the central motive and perspective in making the critique and identifying the theme has been pastoral. In this chapter I want to clarify what is involved in a pastoral perspective, and demonstrate the consistency between the helping stance advocated in the previous chapter and a pastoral stance derived from an understanding of scripture and the tradition of the church.

Various understandings of pastoral care come to us through the tradition of the church, and this variety is reflected in contemporary pastoral literature. A couple of examples serve to demonstrate this. Firstly, Wayne Oates states that:

> Pastoral care can be defined as the Christian pastor's combined fortification and confrontation of persons as persons in times of both emergency crisis and developmental crisis.[1]

Eduard Thurneysen however suggests that:

> Pastoral care occurs within the realm of the church. It commences with the Word and leads back to the Word. It presupposes membership in the body of Christ or has this membership as its purpose. . . (It) can be concerned with nothing else than the proclamation of forgiveness and sanctification of man for God.[2]

Oates' view is representative of those which see pastoral care defined in the attitudes and actions of the carer. Thurneysen represents approaches which focus on the content of pastoral care, seeing it as a practical expression of dogmatic theology within a congregation. Of course these different approaches share a considerable amount of common ground; but there are also significant distinctions between them in practice. The approaches which rely on the person of the pastor to make care pastoral have tended to borrow, quite heavily at times, from the human sciences – psychology, sociology, management theory and so forth. These have provided pastors with rich insights into human problems and with techniques to approach these problem situations. But an outcome of such borrowing has been that the resultant pastoral techniques, resources and language are drawn from the secular sciences and are to some extent alienated from their traditional roots in Christian theology and church practice. On the other hand the approaches which see pastoral care as the application of dogmatic theological insights have frequently lacked flexibility, sensitivity and relevance. Because of an inability or unwillingness to enter into dialogue with the human sciences they have often seemed more concerned with asserting theology's dominance over these disciplines.

Thus there is no clear and generally accepted statement of what it is that makes care pastoral to use in our discussion here. Neither do I want simply to select one of the definitions available in the contemporary literature and use it without further reflection. I believe that a pastoral stance needs more flexibility and creativity than is available within an approach that specifies certain functions as pastoral and sees care as implementing a body of doctrine; but I do not wish to move to a position which implies that everything done by a pastor is necessarily pastoral. Rather I would suggest that a more fruitful approach is to go back to the major images and ideas which have traditionally nurtured and informed pastoral practice, and discover how these might speak to our contemporary understandings of care.[3]

A central image for pastoral care is contained within the name itself; pastor is the Latin word for shepherd, and so pastoral care draws on the tradition of shepherding care which runs throughout scripture. The use of shepherd as a title to indicate the responsibilities of a divine or human leader was common in the ancient world.[4] In biblical literature the title is not applied to any specific human leader, but it is used extensively to describe Yahweh's leadership of his people. The way in which this leadership is envisaged is reflected in passages like Psalm 23 and Ezekiel 34. The latter is an oracle set at the pivotal point of Ezekiel's ministry where his message of judgment becomes a message of deliverance. The shepherding care of Yahweh is contrasted with the self-caring leadership which has brought Israel to ruin. Yahweh's intentions as shepherd of Israel are outlined as follows:

As a shepherd keeps all his flock in view when he stands up in the midst of his scattered sheep, so shall I keep my sheep in view. I shall rescue them from wherever they have been scattered during the mist and darkness . . . I shall feed them in good pasturage . . . I myself will pasture my sheep, I myself will show them where to rest . . . I shall look for the lost one, bring back the stray, bandage the wounded and make the weak strong. I shall watch over the fat and healthy. I shall be a true shepherd to them (Ezek. 34.13–16).

This passage lies behind an oft-quoted definition of shepherding care as the healing, supporting, guiding and reconciling of troubled people.[5] This particular definition focusses largely on individual aspects of care. But it is clear from Ezekiel's description that shepherding care for individuals also has a corporate intention – the rebuilding of the flock – and is linked with a strong concern for justice. God's care points forward into a new future, where a leader (messiah) in the style of King David will emerge once again to shepherd a renewed Israel in this way.[6]

The most direct New Testament expression of the shepherd theme, however, is John 10, where Jesus is portrayed as the true or model shepherd. It would seem that Ezekiel's portrait of God (or the Messiah) as the ideal shepherd, in contrast with the wicked shepherds who have exploited the flock, is the basis for the contrast here of Jesus the ideal shepherd with the pharisees who are characterized as thieves and hirelings.[7] The Johannine passage offers two reasons why Jesus is the true shepherd. The first (in verses 11–13) is that he is the model shepherd because he is willing to die to protect his sheep. The second (in verses 14–16) is that he is the model shepherd because he knows his sheep intimately. Jesus, not the religious leaders, is the shepherd who maintains a covenant relationship with the sheep. The theme of God's intimate knowledge of his people is of course an integral part of the Old Testament shepherding picture; but willingness to die for the sheep is a new feature, introducing elements from the Old Testament descriptions of the Suffering Servant of Yahweh.[8] In his calling, gathering, leading and protecting of his people Jesus displays care which truly reflects the shepherding care of Yahweh.

This shepherding care becomes part of the content of Christian pastoral care in that Christian ministry sees itself as derived from the ministry of Jesus: 'As the Father has sent me so am I sending you' are words of commission from the risen Jesus to his followers (John 20.21). While Jesus risen and with us is the content of the church's proclamation, that proclamation of Jesus as Lord is to include a life-style which exemplifies the values, attitudes and actions of Jesus; his ministry is normative for ours. This is not to say that Christian ministry therefore becomes a mere imitation of events we read about in the Gospel accounts, or that all initiatives taken by the church should be derived directly from the study of the Gospels. Rather, it is our responsibility to see that ministry is consistent with the work of Jesus, based on the same values, reflecting the same attitudes, directed towards the same ends.

In the church, shepherding care is to be expressed in the mutual care of the fellowship: leaders are to care for those they lead; those who are led are to care for their leaders. Thus care is a mutual sharing within the fellowship, extending from within the fellowship to encompass all people.[9] As we have already mentioned, this pastoral care may be described as actions directed towards the healing, guiding, sustaining and reconciling of troubled persons, with these four functions containing the various elements of the biblical shepherding perspective. Clebsch and Jaekle suggest that different historical situations produce different needs and call forth different pastoral responses, so that at any given time one of the four shepherding functions tends to be dominant. For example, in the primitive church the focus of care was upon sustaining people to the end, which was believed to be imminent. In the persecutions pastoral care centred on reconciliation because of the issue created for the Christian community when some professed Christians took the enforced oath to Caesar while others preferred social disadvantage or even martyrdom to perjury. The present time they see as an era of private religion, with personal needs calling forth a pastoral response centred around guidance.[10] I suspect that this in turn is being superseded by a new focus on reconciliation, reflected in the renewed concern among Christians for community life and social justice.

The description of pastoral care in terms of the four shepherding functions of healing, guiding, sustaining and reconciling is particularly useful, even if as noted above these do not represent the full thrust of the shepherding perspective. The biblical emphasis on shepherding care as care forming and sustaining a ministering community which is committed to justice has not been taken sufficiently into account in modern pastoral care. Contemporary pastoral theory and practice has often been too problem-oriented and individualistic in its focus. Another issue raised by Clebsch and Jaekle's historical overview is the strong, almost exclusive identification of pastoral care with the ordained role. Historically, concentrating pastoral responsibility in an ordained shepherd who watches over the congregational flock has often meant understanding pastoral authority as the pastor having power over the congregation. With such an understanding, the mutual aspects of care and corporate responsibility for care are neglected; yet they are a vital part of the biblical shepherding perspective.

It is difficulties such as these which lead me to suggest that the shepherding perspective alone does not provide an adequate basis for pastoral care. While it offers insight into the goals and function of pastoral care it does not provide much guidance as to how decisions about ministry should be made and how pastoral methods might be selected and evaluated. To find answers to questions like these we need to turn to another ministry role which found its fulfilment in Jesus; the Servant of God. This role is not entirely removed from the shepherding motif – there is some indication that the Suffering Servant of Isaiah has influenced Zechariah's portrait of a messianic Shepherd-King – and in John 10 as we noted previously the two images come together in the model shepherd's willingness to offer himself to death.

The Servant theme is a significant strand of both Old and New Testament tradition.[11] The Old Testament source is the four Servant Songs embedded in Isaiah's Book of Consolation (Isa. 42.1–4; 49.1–6; 50.4–9; 52.13–53.12). Here the Servant is shown as a person or a people called to proclaim God's justice, a call which leads progressively into conflict and finally suffering and death which is shown to be redemptive. As the Songs develop there seems to be a shift from a corporate to an individual sense of the Servant's identity.[12]

The Servant Songs and associated texts are basic to the earliest understandings of Jesus (christologies) arrived at by the church, although the idea is so well assimilated that relatively few direct quotations are made in the New Testament documents.[13] The fact that Servant christology is involved in the earliest traditions raises the question as to whether Jesus understood himself in this role of the Servant of God. In the Gospels there certainly are several instances in which Jesus applies the Isaiah passages to himself, and Zimmerli and Jeremias see these as part of the 'bedrock of tradition'.[14] Fuller also sees the Servant role as basic to Jesus' self-understanding, not as a definitive interpretation but as a working concept which guided him in the tasks of his ministry.[15] Cullman maintains that the Servant role, and Jesus' consciousness of it, began at his baptism.[16] Nevertheless, irrespective of the details of Jesus' self-understanding in terms of the Suffering Servant role, it is clear that the early church understood his ministry, and their own, in this way.[17]

In later strata of the New Testament, and in the subsequent development of Christian theology, the Servant motif has been somewhat obscured by the post-Easter emphasis on the divinity of Jesus, an emphasis which has frequently been set in contrast with the Servant role. Christologies based on Phil. 2.5–11 in particular have contributed to this in the way they have used their picture of the pre-existent Christ emptying himself, adopting the Servant role, and subsequently being exalted, by implication stripping off the earthly disguise of the Servant to reveal the Christ within. Such kenosis (emptying) christologies have been used at various times in the church's history in an attempt to resolve the apparent paradox of the dual nature of Christ.[18] In this attempt they have been unsuccessful; but they have kept alive the Servant theme in New Testament theology. J. A. T. Robinson summarizes the situation in this way:

> As an exercise in showing how a divine person or a semi-divine being or even a heavenly man could 'become' a man or 'experience life as a man' without ceasing to be essentially other than a man, I believe it (kenosis theory) represents a fruitless expenditure of theological ingenuity. But if it is used, as I think the New Testament uses it, to show how a man, and an utterly humiliated man, could nevertheless *be* the self-expression of the wisdom and the power, the freedom and the triumph, of the love that 'moves the sun and the stars', then it provides a marvellously rich vein for theological exploration. For it declares the profound truth that 'the form of a Servant' is not a derogation from or even a modification of the glory of God, but precisely the fullest expression of that glory as love.[19]

The same point is made by P. T. Forsyth and C. F. D. Moule among others:[20] the human limitations of Jesus are to be seen as a positive expression of his divinity rather than a temporary curtailment of it. The ministry of Jesus is not merely a prelude to Easter, but an expression of the Easter message; and by implication the Servant theme is not merely of historical interest but a theme which is to inform the proclamation and life-style of the church.

Further insight into how the servant role shaped and directed Jesus' ministry can be derived from the Synoptic Gospels. Each writer begins his record of Jesus' public ministry with an account of his baptism and wilderness temptation (Matt. 3.13–4:11; Mark 1.9–13; Luke 3.21–22; 4.1–13). Contained in these accounts is the implication that it is here at the beginning of his ministry that Jesus adopts the Servant role. Each account establishes the link with Isaiah's Servant in the words of the voice from heaven, quoting from the first Servant Song. Matthew then proceeds to give a detailed account of the wilderness experience, in which Jesus affirms the call proclaimed at his baptism, and chooses his mode of ministry.

He presents Jesus as confronted with three specific temptations, the first two of which are prefaced by a testing of his baptismal call (*If you are the Son of God. . .*) The temptations raise the central question of how his Sonship is to be understood and expressed in ministry. In response to these Jesus makes certain choices. He chooses self-limitation. He rejects a ministry based on miraculous proofs. He chooses to realize his Lordship not by coercion but by love. Thus he will use his ministry to feed others rather than himself; he will not be diverted into meeting needs in a way which ignores our need for God as well as our need for bread. He will proclaim God's justice and salvation – but he will leave the responsibility and freedom to respond with the people who hear his message. He invites people to freedom, and he will not use means inconsistent with his goal. In each choice Jesus asserts his dependence upon God and not upon his own powers. He chooses total obedience. It is thus that he is true God, accurately reflecting to us God's attitudes and desires. And it is also why he is true Man, because in his obedience he shows us what we can and ought to be.[21]

The method of ministry that Jesus chooses in the wilderness is that of the Suffering Servant, and his public ministry follows this pattern. It begins with the proclamation of God's love and justice and continues through conflict to the redemptive suffering of the cross. Conflict arises both around the content of his proclamation and around his style of ministry. There is tension between his understanding of himself and the expectations which people place upon him, and an examination of this tension can spell out a number of practical aspects of the Servant role.

Perhaps the clearest examples are provided by Jesus' responses to the titles by which people addressed him.[22] To the rich young ruler who comes up to him and begins 'Good Master, what must I do to inherit eternal life?', Jesus replies, 'Why do you call me good. . .?' (Mark 10.17f.). To the man who demands that he adjudicate in a dispute over an inheritance Jesus responds, 'Who made me a judge over you?' (Luke 12.14). To the governor at his trial, in answer to the question 'Are you the King of the Jews?', Jesus replies, 'The words are yours' (Matt. 27.11). Even when Jesus acknowledges Peter's recognition of him as the Christ he immediately has cause to reprimand Peter for dissociating this title from the meaning and content which Jesus gives to it (Matt. 16.13–23). Jesus will not give even tacit assent to the titles by which we try to enlist him in our cause or interpret him solely in the categories of the past. We who try to categorize him find that we must take responsibility for our words and actions, and so are faced by the question which he asked his disciples after they had presented him with other people's estimates of his identity; 'But you – who do you say that I am?' (Matt. 16.15).

These encounters give some important insights into what it means to be a servant. In particular they dispose of the popular misconception that Christian service means doing whatever other people ask of us. Jesus in fact shows that he is God's servant because he is not at the beck and call of anyone else. His self-understanding and his actions in ministry are based on God's call, not other people's opinions or wishes. As God's servant he is committed to meeting human need, but the way he does so places that need in its broadest context. He deals with the whole person; he is not content to cure bodies alone, he ministers to mind and spirit as well. Neither will he allow questions of the spirit to remain separate from the rest of life; the religious question is answered in terms of relationships, money, practical justice. His task is to minister to people's real needs, not pander to their wants. Thus an important aspect of the Servant role is confrontation, refusing to 'assist' people by meeting desires which distract them from the fundamental issues of life and faith.

Attempts to objectify and keep him safely categorized are resisted by Jesus with an authority which is based in his call. He does not, however, use this authority to control another person's perception of him. In relationships he offers to others the freedom he requires of them in return. His care is expressed in helping people to face reality and make their own decisions about it. He will not support or condone the inauthentic defences which lead others to want to contain and categorize him; but neither will he attack those defences other than by his own example of freedom, inviting the other person to come out from behind those defences to meet him. Jesus as the Servant of God raises questions about our assumptions and opens up new possibilities through his own example. He claims to work and speak for God, and those who see him must judge the truth of this for themselves. He refuses to plead his case, or produce signs for the sceptical. Through him we may choose to see God, and thus ourselves, in a new way. Alternatively we may reject his testimony and try to rid ourselves of him. Helplessness and suffering are thus possible outcomes of the Servant's obedience and proclamation. They are potential within the choices made by Jesus at the beginning of his ministry.

The helplessness which was present as a possibility in Jesus' wilderness decision becomes actual in Gethsemane. Here Jesus, in agony, renews the choices made in the wilderness, and by reason of those choices is delivered to judgment and to Calvary. The Servant is called to obey, to proclaim, and to suffer. Jesus is abandoned by his followers to the physical helplessness of torture and crucifixion, and to the mental and spiritual helplessness of abandonment by God, expressed in his cry of dereliction. He dies powerless and helpless, his death a direct result of the decisions taken in the wilderness and re-affirmed throughout his ministry. Yet it is at this point of utter helplessness that God brings new meaning, revealing what he has been doing. The helplessness of Calvary is at once the truth about our human situation and a pointer beyond to the grace of God who is involved in the suffering and who brings meaning out of it. The glory of God is shown not in contrast with helplessness, but through it.

Our ministry, if modelled on that of Jesus, will also encounter suffering and helplessness; not that we will aim at this, but we will recognize it as a risk involved in pursuing and proclaiming a vision of God's love and justice. The Suffering Servant is not in search of suffering, but has a vision of reality and a hope in God's justice which makes suffering an unavoidable part of his quest. It is the vision, the goal, which sustains his ministry in suffering; suffering of itself is not seen as a vindication of his ministry, neither does suffering guarantee the result. We cannot use the fact of our suffering to prove the validity of our care – all too often we suffer because we have tried to meet our own needs through a helping relationship, or have failed to distinguish between what we are actually called to do and all the other things we have been asked to do. Neither can we use helplessness as a technique, over-extending or immobilizing ourselves as a matter of policy in the hope that God (or one of his representatives) will rescue us. God's grace cannot be manipulated in this way; he does not provide grace to excuse us from responsibility. Suffering and helplessness are not to be sought for their own sake, but they will be encountered in any authentic ministry. To try to organize a helping relationship so that the risk of suffering is eliminated, or to withdraw as soon as helplessness threatens, is to frustrate any possibility of real ministry.

While suffering is not to be sought or avoided, neither is it to be regarded as merely a necessary evil. Entering into another person's suffering is one of the greatest challenges and opportunities of the pastoral task. It is frequently out of suffering that new hope and meaning emerge; and it is often out of our own suffering that we learn how to help in the first place. Discovering that our suffering and loss can be entered into and transcended frees us to minister. Discovering how our suffering is transcended saves us from urging upon others inappropriate palliative solutions which are at best a distraction from the underlying issues. We can help because we are witnesses to the fact that hope can be found through suffering. Both our words and our presence express this. But we will also convey the fact that the experience of loss must be entered into, for it is only in experiencing the reality of loss that it can be transcended. The pastoral helper offers both comfort and challenge. To people facing pain and loss we demonstrate a hope for wholeness which is based in our own experience. We also refuse to support any wish to avoid the painful reality of loss, for avoidance leads sooner or later to illness and despair.

This pastoral helping role has been described by Henri Nouwen in terms of ministry:

> A minister is not a doctor whose primary task is to take away pain. Rather, he deepens the pain to a level where it can be shared. When someone comes with his loneliness to the minister, he can only expect that his loneliness will be understood and felt, so that he no longer has to run away from it but can accept it as an expression of his basic human condition. . .
>
> Perhaps the main task of the minister is to prevent people from suffering for the wrong reasons. Many people suffer because of the false supposition on which they have based their lives. That supposition is that there should be no fear or loneliness, no confusion or doubt. But these sufferings can only be dealt with creatively when they are understood as wounds integral to our human condition. Therefore ministry is a very confronting service. It does not allow people to live with illusions of immortality and wholeness. It keeps reminding others that they are mortal and broken, but also that with the recognition of their condition, liberation starts.
>
> No minister can save anyone. He can only offer himself as a guide to fearful people. Yet, paradoxically, it is precisely in this guidance that the first signs of hope become visible. . . When we become aware that we do not have to escape our pains, but that we can mobilize them in a common search for life, those very pains are transformed from expressions of despair into signs of hope.[23]

Trust in God is basic to the servant role: trust in God's call gives identity and a sense of purpose, while God's grace must be trusted in witnessing to wholeness and speaking of hope. The servant's task is to prepare the way to wholeness through personal example and through establishing a relationship which offers support and opens up ultimate questions. Healing or wholeness however cannot be guaranteed; it is a gift from God, mediated by a servant perhaps but not in that servant's possession in such a way that he can deliver it.

The event which initiates and enables the servant's trust is Calvary. Here our human helplessness is given a new potential meaning. Through the ages our human responses to our helplessness have taken one of two major forms. Either we have sought to overcome it by our own efforts, attempting to control God through ritual and sacrifice. Or we have interpreted our helplessness as being inevitable under the apparent capriciousness of a remote and disinterested God, becoming depressed, cynical and resigned. Calvary, however, shows us a third way; hope in the grace of God. Here we see the true nature of God's involvement with and control of circumstances which are beyond our control. His control does not avert tragedy, but brings meaning out of an event which is to our human perception an unmitigated disaster. To perceive this meaning is to experience grace. At Calvary we see that God is uncontrollable – but not unpredictable. His attitude towards us is constant; he accepts us unreservedly as we are. The paradox of grace lies in the fact that our perception of God's attitude, which comes to us as grace, allows us to live as if in control of our uncontrollable circumstances. The circumstances themselves are not changed, but through our new relationship with God we see them differently. Certain qualities are now perceived to be of greater significance than others. Beauty, goodness and truth are recognized as signs of God's transcendence, while the evil, pain and suffering with which they co-exist are seen to be transient. The perspective of grace enables us to choose to hope in the midst of suffering and helplessness.

Jesus' task as Servant was to call into being a community of people to witness to God's grace. This he did by his ministry, and especially in his submission to death. The mission committed to his church is to be that community of grace. The church is to serve the world as a witness to God's grace; it is to demonstrate that grace within its corporate life, despite its human fragmentation; it is to call other people into the community to participate in that life. Care has the purpose of nurturing the community, equipping the members for service, supporting them in ministry. Pastoral care interpenetrates and supports all aspects of the church's life in the world.

The purpose of this discussion has been to develop criteria distinguishing a pastoral perspective, and while I do not intend to offer a formal definition of pastoral care I would suggest that a pastoral perspective contains at least these elements:

1. Pastoral care is the work of the whole church (not the clergy

alone). Its model is the shepherding-serving ministry of Jesus which is committed to his church.

2. Pastoral care occurs within the community of the church and reaches out from that community. It is mutual care, aiming at growth to maturity, not merely the resolution of problems. The purpose of care is to call people into community as participating members, and to equip them for ministry. Care thus offers commitment in a continuing relationship.

3. Pastoral care is a stance or attitude which expresses itself in helping acts. The intention of these acts is the healing, guiding, supporting and reconciling of people in all aspects of their lives. Pastoral care as a discipline, however, knows that it can only witness to the reality of health, guidance, support and reconciliation; these are not the gift of a pastor, but gifts of God's grace. Thus pastoral care recognizes its preliminary nature. It prepares the way of the Lord, depending on God's grace as well as proclaiming it.

4. Pastoral care is concerned with the meaning of human experience. Its task is not to deliver answers or interpretations so much as to assist in uncovering them. A pastoral relationship thus involves a commitment to another person in his or her search for truth. This commitment is itself a witness to truth.

Any one of these criteria does not uniquely define pastoral care, but together they represent a concept of care which stands in contrast to many contemporary understandings. As a particular example we consider the current hospital model of care[24] which could be described by criteria like these:

1. Care is a function best carried out by professional helpers, and can be delivered by non-needy staff to needy patients. The caring relationship is not recognized as mutual, but is confined to the professional person's area of expertise.

2. Care is best (that is, most efficiently) provided by taking individuals from the context of their everyday relationships and bringing them into an institution for treatment. The caring relationship thus offered does not imply any commitment beyond that of seeking a solution to the immediate presenting problem.

3. The goal of care is the relief of physical symptoms and, if possible, cure of the disease process producing the symptoms. The focus is upon eliminating disease more than upon promoting health.

4. Care does not need to explore the meaning of illness for a particular patient; it is enough to effect a cure.

The helping role issuing from this hospital model of care has already been outlined in the previous chapter's discussion of the doctor-patient relationship. Clearly these criteria are in tension with the pastoral criteria outlined above. Perhaps the contrast is a little overdrawn; although there are certainly harsher critical summaries of the medical model of care than the perspective I am offering here.[25] A more pertinent observation would be that I am comparing here what pastoral care ought to be with what medical care actually is. Nevertheless, although the contrast may be qualified by considerations like this, it can be seen that there are basic differences between the concept of care which underlies modern medical practice and the concept of care which is drawn from the pastoral heritage of the church.

We are now in a position to test the claim made at the beginning of this chapter; that the helping stance developed in chapter 2 is consistent with a pastoral perspective. You will remember that that stance included characteristics such as these: proper care must give attention to the needs of the whole person – physical, mental, spiritual and social – and take seriously the person's perspective in assessing those needs; that the goals of care, and the details of the helping relationship, are negotiable between carer and dying person; and that consequently the helping relationship is recognized to be mutual. The helper must look at the limits to his own competence and his own needs within the relationship; this recognition makes him vulnerable. He must also be prepared to distinguish between his professional role and his personal identity, being willing to enter into a helping relationship which can still continue even when specific professional skills are no longer relevant or helpful.

It should be clear from the foregoing discussion that these character-istics correlate much more closely with pastoral criteria than with the current medical model of care. Wholistic concern, person-centred care, and a mutual helping relationship which involves the helper beyond any purely professional functions, are pastoral emphases which are neglected in or negated by the medical model. Negotiation over control (the sharing of power) is also more possible within a pastoral stance than the medical model which requires the patient to relinquish responsibility (accept powerlessness) in institutionally-prescribed ways.

Given then that the helping stance of chapter 2 is grounded more in pastoral than in medical concepts, there are two further issues we need to explore. The first is whether pastoral insights can clarify or extend the model, remembering that it has been developed to this point out of clinical observations and helplessness theory, not from a full set of pastoral criteria. The second issue arises because of the model's grounding in pastoral rather than medical concepts. Applying the model to terminal care must therefore mean more than simply revising or re-ordering practices derived from the medical model; it implies a re-examination of some of the basic concepts of terminal care.

It seems to me that the pastoral criteria outlined earlier enable us to augment the helplessness model in several areas. The nature of authority and power in the helping relationship; expectations of care; and the place of values in care are particular examples to which we turn. It is also around these issues that the conceptual differences between pastoral and medical models are sharpest.

Authority and power

The medical model of care allows the helper to define a person's needs in physical terms and assume control over physical care while disclaiming responsibility for other aspects of need. The helper's authority to do this comes from a status achieved through training, and is expressed in power to require compliance with medical guidelines. We have already seen in fact that this focus on physical care, especially in institutional contexts, adversely affects the other components of a person's need.

Pastoral care recognizes a responsibility to care for the whole person, and this care may be expressed in a variety of helping acts addressed to the physical, mental, social and spiritual needs of the person. Fundamental to the pastoral relationship is the understanding that while authority and power may be mediated through the relationship, the source of that authority and power lies outside it. By this I mean that both parties in the relationship are under the same ultimate authority, and there are no grounds for one to assume control of the other. Nor can one partner in the relationship guarantee to the other that healing, or reconciliation, or salvation will come about. No one person is in control of these things; they are gifts of God's grace. We must wait and hope that he will mediate them through the relationship.

Thus as a helper I may be able to offer specific acts of service to a dying person (medication, a bed pan, a psalm or a prayer) but I cannot guarantee that any act of service will meet his underlying needs. If in fact I act as if I can deliver healing or reconciliation or salvation then I will probably block the pathway of grace because I will be drawing attention to myself and my unrealistic self-understanding rather than directing attention to God as the source of grace. Similarly, as a dying person I must learn to accept acts of service graciously, but not look for salvation or rescue in those acts. I have a responsibility to use the support and care I am receiving in order to search out the meaning of this part of my life; I cannot expect to be given the answer by someone else.

As a professional helper I will have access to information and skills which give me power. The critical question in care is how I use that power; to serve other people, or to control their behaviour and treatment. In pastoral perspective, a proper use of power is that I use it to release the other person. I will not use my power to block his access to information or people he needs. Neither will I use my power to blast through his defences if he is not yet ready to face his situation. Rather I will offer a relationship in which the other person can find freedom to explore and understand. But I will not attempt to control his life, nor will I allow him to make of me either a scapegoat or a saviour. Because my authority comes from my self-understanding as God's servant I will limit any idolatrous urges to act as a saviour so that I may point more accurately to the real source of power and grace. It is probably worth stressing the point that acting in this way is not adopting a passive attitude; passivity is the situation in which I am unaware of or unwilling to use my power. As a servant, however, I am aware of my power for both healing and destruction, and choose to use it for the former purpose.

Expectations

A pastoral understanding of a helping relationship reminds me that I cannot take full responsibility – either credit or blame – for the outcome of that relationship. I am not responsible to cure a person so much as to see that it is possible for healing to take place. I am not responsible for the meaning that person chooses to affirm; but I am responsible to see that he has a chance to choose a meaning in the first place through the freedom offered in our relationship. I may of course hope that he will find a truth congruent with that by which I live; but I cannot do more than witness to that truth. Thus I expect to play my part in the relationship, accepting the outcome whether it be joy or sorrow, affirmation or helplessness. And I expect that I will learn from each pastoral encounter more about myself and our shared human condition. I am responsible to reflect upon my work and relationships.

Caring and values

Any system of care is based on a set of values, and the helping roles assigned by the system require helpers to incarnate those values. If the system's values are inconsistent with the values and needs of the people within it, fundamental problems arise.

This appears to be the case when the general acute-care hospital medical model of care is applied to terminal care. The medical model has in effect promoted value statements like 'Death is the worst thing that can happen to anyone' and 'Everyone must be given every possible chance to escape from death.' Within a cure-oriented institution it can be argued that these values issue in appropriate helping strategies. Personally I would not agree with that argument, but even given agreement with that point of view it is still clear that in terminal care many medically-desirable helping roles and strategies are obviously or subtly inappropriate to the patients' needs and wishes. The medical model's valuing of a helper on the basis of his technical abilities more than pastoral qualities contributes to this dilemma.

A model of care derived from pastoral criteria, however, places a high value on the person. It endeavours to respect the values and needs of patients, and it focusses attention on the personal integrity and self-understanding of the helper. As well as having technical skills appropriate to a patient's needs a helper needs to be able to share the other person's humanity, being open to the same sort of questions and searching which the other is undergoing. Thus a helper needs to be someone who is committed to establishing and affirming a world view which takes adequate account of both life and death.

A pastoral perspective also raises questions about values like those ascribed above to the medical model. Is death really the worst thing that can happen to someone? From a pastoral perspective we might answer 'no'. It is worse never to live; never to discover who you are and what you are called to do with your life or to whom you are to belong. A pastoral perspective also raises questions of justice: what in fact is a just distribution of health care resources? Do our current health care practices use these resources equitably?

In the following chapters we will bring a pastoral perspective to bear firstly upon the specific issues of helping dying people to hope and to find an appropriate death. We then turn to a discussion of ways in which institutional structures and professional roles might be revised better to incorporate a pastoral dimension of care.

4

· *Hope* ·

Hope is a word used frequently in writing about terminal care. However, what this hope might be, and how it might be expressed, is seldom discussed. In everyday language hope refers to an idea, a vision or a wish concerning the future, an expectation of something which is desired; but in medical usage the word seems to be limited implicitly to hope for recovery or survival. The wish to die, for example, is seldom recognized as hope, even though it may be a person's desire for the future. The object of hope in most clinical literature is a future in which the patient has been restored to physical health, or is at least still living.

In actual clinical practice two operational ideas about hope can be distinguished. The first of these is that hope is something which patients retain as long as sufficient information is withheld from them ('Nothing should be said to take away the patient's hope'). The second, usually a fall-back position introduced when patients have inferred or been told their prognoses, is that hope is a belief system which can be delivered in propositional form (preferably by a chaplain).

I believe that both these pragmatic views of hope are quite inadequate; indeed that they are a travesty of real hope, hopelessness masquerading as hope. Hope is not the same thing as wishful thinking or unfounded optimism, nor is it merely a set of concepts to be given intellectual assent. Rather, hope has its birth in a realistic assessment of our situation, and is grounded in our experiences and the values by which we live. I think that this can be demonstrated by looking at the way hope is formed and broken down and re-formed in dying people, both those who are hopeful and those who are in despair.

At the beginning of an illness hope for recovery is usually common to doctor, patient and family. Changes occur if the illness progresses and is diagnosed as terminal. The doctor's perspective alters to seeing the case as hopeless, for nothing more can be done to bring about recovery. The patient and family, however, may continue to hope for recovery, either through ignorance of the doctor's changed perspective, or because they hope for some extraordinary intervention: an act of God, a new medical discovery, a cure through alternative methods of treatment. In this case their hope has become hope in spite of the evidence. It is a hope seldom shared by medically-trained personnel, but it is nevertheless found in most terminally-ill people. As Elisabeth Kübler-Ross remarks, 'even the most accepting, the most realistic patients left the possibility open for some cure, for the discovery of a new drug, or the last-minute success in a research project'.[1] This hope for recovery however is usually residual; it is seldom the major component of a person's hope towards the end of a terminal illness.

The diagnosis of a terminal illness and the doctor's loss of hope for recovery often leads to the abrupt introduction of a different sort of hope, the hope for immortality. The chaplain or a local minister may be called in, more or less as part of the treatment, in the expectation that he will be able to bring about a change in the patient's hope from a this-worldly expectation (recovery) to an other-worldly expectation (immortality). And such a change may indeed occur, although introducing religious hope as an antidote for medical hopelessness takes little account of the way hope grows, and assumes an unfortunate dichotomy between medicine as dealing with life and religion as dealing with death.

We will begin to look at the process by which hope for recovery can change in the face of death by considering the possible endpoints of this process. I will distinguish two in particular which I will call affirmation and resignation. The former is based on hope and is able to find and affirm creative possibilities in the face of death. The latter is based on despair, seeing death as an end with no more beginnings possible. I want to qualify this distinction by emphasizing that these two positions are not to be seen as alternatives so much as endpoints of a continuum of attitudes; most dying people demonstrate mixed responses, although overall they will incline one way or the other. It is also important to reiterate that many people do not move much beyond the early stages of the dying process, and never really grapple with the questions about meaning which enable them to reach an essentially stable attitude to their dying. In this discussion I am concerned with what is possible; some of the reasons why people do not achieve the potential endpoint of affirmation will become clearer from what follows.

From my experience of hopeful and hopeless dying people, and from first-person written accounts, I would like to suggest some basic characteristics of affirmation and resignation. Some major features of affirmation are:

1. We have a realistic knowledge of our situation.
2. The focus of our attention is upon our quality of life; living, learning, appreciating. We are open to new experiences and some new relationships; our perspective on life is broader than our immediate situation.
3. We are peaceful, relaxed, able to live in the moment.
4. We can affirm our life in the face of death. We see a meaning for life, memory being the basis for this perception. Our hope is personal and meaningful, having both concrete and transcendent aspects.

Some major features of resignation are:

1. We have a realistic knowledge of our situation.
2. Our focus is upon the quantity of life remaining to us and our approaching end. Our interest centres on our immediate situation or predicament; we tend to be passive and withdrawn.
3. Our attitude is stoical, courageously despairing. There is tension as we wait for the inevitable.
4. We perceive the irony of life in the face of death. Life seems to be ultimately meaningless, and this dictates to our memory, conditioning what we recall. Despair emerges, generalizing from our own situation to colour our view of the whole world.

This description of course makes a clear distinction between affirmation and resignation. It is based on characteristics of people who have been predominantly affirming or predominantly resigned. As noted already, in practice these characteristics hardly ever appear in such clear-cut forms; most people show a mixture of attitudes. However, I have distinguished the endpoints in this way because if we are to describe the process leading from hope for recovery to the final state of hopeful affirmation or resigned acceptance of death, we need to use a relatively simple model. Otherwise, describing the complex interpenetration of hope, denial, affirmation and resignation which is a dying person's experience would be a well-nigh impossible task. I have thus chosen these simplified endpoints, and in what follows I will develop a simplified description for the process itself.

I will begin with a model put forward by Avery Weisman, a psychiatrist who has described the dying process in terms of the variety of defences used by a person to shield himself from the knowledge of his imminent death.[2] Weisman groups these defences into categories of denial, suggesting that three levels or orders can be distinguished.[3]

First order: denying the primary facts of the illness, the symptoms.

Second order: denying the inferences to be drawn from the symptoms.

Third order: denying the possibility of extinction, of death being the end of existence.

In his description each level of denial has a corresponding level of acceptance. The breakdown of first-order denial, which admits the reality of illness into consciousness, opens up a first-order acceptance, which is at this stage limited by second-order denial. Similarly the breakdown of second-order denial leads to second-order acceptance, admitting the possibility that the symptoms recognized in first-order acceptance may actually be those of a terminal illness. Again, this second-order acceptance is limited by third-order denial. Once third-order denial has broken down, however, all the possibilities of the situation are available for scrutiny; denial no longer screens certain aspects of reality from our perception.

I want to extend Weisman's model by suggesting that various levels of hope can be associated with his levels of denial and acceptance.

Weisman suggests that terminal illness often begins with first-order denial, denial of the symptoms themselves. Certainly delay in seeking medical advice is well-documented for a number of diseases, cancer in particular.[4] However, such denial cannot stand too much contact with reality, and can be maintained for a long period only by retreat into fantasy. When first-order denial operates there is no place for hope in the face of illness and death. We see ourselves as healthy, and we cannot contemplate a change in that situation; in essence we think of ourselves as immortal. Our society, however, actively attacks this level of denial once symptoms of an illness emerge; public health education and pressure from family and friends will soon break it down. It is with the breakdown of this first-order denial that first-order acceptance appears, shown in the recognition of our symptoms and of our need for help. With this acceptance, a first-order hope may also be formed. This is a hope for recovery, for a return to our former state of health. At this point no other possibilities are envisaged. There are several ways in which this hope can appear. It may emerge out of a period of despair which follows the breakdown of denial; we may make a straightforward transition from admitting the reality of our illness to affirming a hope for recovery; it may even be that admitting illness plunges us into despair and resignation from which we do not emerge. The hope which we affirm in first-order acceptance, however, is simple. The reality of symptoms is admitted, help is sought, but second-order denial still operates to exclude from consciousness all possibilities other than recovery or indefinitely prolonged illness. It is in the former that our hope is invested.

This next stage, second-order denial and first-order hope, tends to be supported heavily by hospitals and by society in general. First-order denial as we have already noted is actively confronted for it keeps a person from becoming a patient. Second-order denial in contrast is encouraged, because it gives medical access to the symptoms while suppressing fear of death and the difficult questions which attend that fear. At this stage, with hope understood solely in terms of hope for recovery, the will to live and the wish to die are seen as antitheses. This perception is usually shared by patient, doctor and family. Because of the consensus, it can be very hard for a patient to move beyond this stage. While the people around a dying person cannot control his thoughts and attitudes, they nevertheless can influence them. If in order to support the hope for recovery they deliberately control information and the level of relationship offered, then the dying person's assumptions and perceptions are affected. Because he cannot obtain a realistic knowledge of his situation, his attempts to test reality will give misleading, or at least ambiguous, results.

Our social preference for second-order denial linked with first-order hope means that the breakdown of second-order denial is the critical transition if hope is to continue to develop in terminal illness. By coming to accept not only that we are ill but that our illness may be terminal, we open ourselves to possibilities inherent in dying from this particular illness. However, because many of the people around us will not accept as a legitimate hope our wishes concerning the mode of our dying, we may be unable to explore and appropriate these possibilities for our dying as part of our hope. It is this lack of support that can make the breakdown of second-order denial such a difficult time. In fact, the second-order acceptance which emerges from this breakdown commonly issues in resignation and despair; for the withdrawal of community is particularly destructive of hope. If all our hope has been invested in recovery, then that hope may virtually be destroyed by the new perception of second-order acceptance. A hope which can go beyond a mere insistence upon recovery needs to be found. If possibilities for dying cannot be faced and explored, such a hope cannot emerge. And even when it does, this second-order hope will still refuse, through the operation of third-order denial, to contemplate the possibility of extinction in death, even though death is now seen as a possibility. Third-order denial still screens off the fundamental questions of meaning which can be affirmed in the face of death.

At this stage of second-order hope we may quite realistically choose to hope for death rather than crave life at any price; the will to live and the wish to die become two versions of hope. Most terminally-ill people do seem to reach this second stage where such a hope becomes possible; but those who can find a meaningful hope which they are allowed to affirm are distressingly few. When second-order hope does appear it is more varied than the single-minded first-order hope for recovery. It has more short term elements, and is far less absolute than the first-order hope which required increasing support from denial. Now we may simply hope to die with dignity; or we may hope for the continuing success of our children; or that our partners will find the support they need; or that our life's contribution will continue to be remembered and found useful. These simple, personal hopes will sustain us.

All too frequently family and hospital staff will not allow these hopes to be articulated. An expressed wish to die in a certain way will often be heard as despair by staff and family. A somewhat tentative statement such as 'If I do have to go at least I hope it will be as peaceful as it was for old Bill last night' is more than likely to be met with the response 'Don't be morbid' than with the recognition that here is a person beginning to explore possibilities for his own dying. Yet it is often in the simple everyday exchanges like this that staff and family indicate their own wishes for recovery or prolongation of life. These imposed first-order hopes can ultimately crush a patient's emerging second-order hopes as the burden of unwanted treatment drags on or as isolation increases because an honest sharing of feelings and attitudes with family and staff is no longer possible. There are numerous case-studies showing the destruction or near-destruction of a patient's capacity to hope through the insistence of family or staff on an inappropriate, absolute hope for recovery.[5]

The second-order hope outlined above is still supported by third-order denial; the possibility that death will be the end for us has not yet really been faced. Thus it is the breakdown of third-order denial which leads on to the crucial question of meaning, the necessity of us choosing a stance concerning the ultimate meaning of life. Third-order hope will affirm such a stance. It will also have many of the elements of second-order and even first-order hope, but it will not require support by denial. It is a mature hope which can examine all possibilities, and out of them choose what will be hoped for. This mature hope is supported and validated by memory. Experiences in the past have proved to us certain things about the trustworthiness of life – events have worked for good even though life has been at many points difficult and confusing. This basic trustworthiness of life, and the meaning found through reflection on the past, is the basis for our present hope and trust. To use a theological term, our memory functions as salvation history: we look back and say in effect, 'I was in trouble and was delivered from it here, and here, and again here in my life. Now I once again face the unknown, but I believe that somehow it will be all right.' While what we hope for in the present may have some elements of hope in spite of the circumstances, it is nevertheless grounded in past reality, not in denial. People with this mature hope are able to accept themselves and the validity of their experiences. Their lives are moving towards integration, wholeness, unlike the lives of people in despair where the immediate predicament has swamped all previously-held meaning and perspective.

To say that third-order hope, mature hope must confront the possibility of extinction is not to say that mature hope cannot include hope for the personal survival of death. Certainly it may; but this hope will be chosen in full recognition that it is a faith claim, not an unarguable certainty. In this way a third-order hope for life after death is distinguished from a second-order hope which uses the idea of immortality to avoid confronting the possibility of real dying. The second-order hope needs denial to support it, and the tension of denial is frequently shown in the fervour, almost desperation, with which such people will declaim their certainty about details of eternity. Third-order hope, however, needs no support from denial; it has looked at the possibilities and chosen from among them. Third-order hope thus presents as simple, personal, and free in comparison with the attitudes of those who affirm ultimate meanings from a position supported by denial. Nor should it be assumed that a lack of any belief or hope in after-life leads inevitably to hopelessness and despair. It need not; there certainly are people who find a hope to sustain them even though they have no hope for personal survival. Even so, that hope usually contains some elements which go beyond or transcend the person's death; the hope that the cause to which they have given their life will prosper and eventually triumph, for example, or the hope that the values they cherish will continue in their children and their children's children.

As I indicated above, this outline of the process of hope is simplified, but I believe that the major features it discloses are essentially correct. I would emphasize in particular these:

1. A lasting or mature hope is formed through a process of testing and clarifying reality; that is, through struggle. Hope and denial are antitheses, not fellow travellers. Reality is at the core of this hope, which is conscious of the whole range of possibilities, yet chooses to invest itself in particular selected outcomes.

2. Mature hope is open to possibility, and does not insist on its own solution. By this I mean that the actual details of a mature hope are not as important as its trust that, whatever may be hoped for, that which actually happens will be for the best. This hope appears as a personal trust more than as commitment to details of a plan for the future. I find it difficult to express this fundamental aspect in any way other than by saying that it is a trust in God, even though the person who holds it may have no formal belief or religious affiliation.

3. Mature hope is characterized by an ability to wait. Encountering reality takes time, and involves suffering and confusion as some immature hopes are broken down and fresh options appear. Mature hope can emerge from this process; it will not, however, emerge if the person is not prepared to wait, but insists on achieving immediate certainty at every point of confusion.

4. The content of mature hope is strongly personal, focussed among other things on the welfare of people or causes which have been of real significance in the person's life. Again, this is not saying that mature hope may not be linked into an established system of belief. The person may espouse the values of Christianity (or Marxism or atheism for that matter). But these values will have personal significance. They will be internalized, acted upon, lived out in the person's life.

Our discussion so far has been within the context of terminal illness, but even so attention has been directed beyond this into the quality of the dying person's life and the values on which his life has been based. It is something of a truism, although not always remembered in discussions about terminal care, that a person brings to dying the resources by which he has lived. If he has not found any particular meaning or purpose in living, he is unlikely to find it in dying. If his life has had meaning and purpose this will be tested in dying, but he will have a lifetime of experience and achievement as a foundation for this testing, and values which hopefully can be re-affirmed even in the changed circumstances, thus becoming the basis for mature hope.

This highlights the fact that learning to hope and preparing to die are things which we do as we learn to live. Coming to terms with reality and our human finitude is at the core of all human development. We are confronted with our finitude in many ways: through limits we experience to our physical and personal capacities; through anxiety; through illness; through the deaths of others. The decisions that we make and the behaviour we choose in these situations shape our lives, and determine whether we live authentically (with a realistic awareness of our mortality) or inauthentically (ignoring or denying our mortality). To live authentically is to be prepared for our own death, even though it is only in one's own dying that death can be fully apprehended existentially.[6] Encountering and being involved in the deaths of others cannot face us completely with our own death; but it can give to us insight and hope. It can widen our perception of reality, remind us of our finitude, and lead us to the hope that in our own dying we may achieve the maturity and hopefulness we have seen in others. A hope like this has yet to be tested by the imminent reality of our own dying, but it will be a foundation on which we can build towards affirmation rather than despair in our dying time.

If in our lives we have not faced up to our mortality, then the experience of dying will issue a profound challenge to our existing values and hopes. We may have no answers, no resources with which to meet the questions posed by discovering that our lives will soon end. We may be faced with a choice between clinging on to hopes which are no longer appropriate, or allowing the reality of our situation to break these hopes down with little or no prospect of learning to hope again. It is out of situations like this that the inadequate versions of hope arise. A fundamental problem in the process of hope occurs when the hope for recovery, a legitimate hope especially in the early stages of illness, is made absolute; patient, family or staff cling to it because every other alternative is seen or felt to be hopeless, unbearable. If this is the case, as illness progresses the initially-legitimate hope becomes tyrannical, demanding that all other possibilities be denied and that the person stop looking clearly at reality. A hope has become the vehicle of hopelessness. It is now pathological, manipulative, refusing to examine possibilities other than recovery, imposing a false clarity on the available evidence, selecting signs and requesting responses from others to reinforce the hope for recovery while denying indicators to the contrary. It cannot weigh the evidence or wait for confusion to be resolved. The person who holds this sort of hope is trapped within it, neurotically driven to shore up the denial which supports it. In contrast, real hope in the same situation can wait for clarity. Its wishes are clear; they are grounded in personal reality, and so such a hope does not have to distort reality to conform to itself. It probably will include within itself hope for recovery, but it will not be committed exclusively to this component. To use a distinction based on Freud's model of personality, the false hope is an id phenomenon, trapped in the id's repetition compulsion and its demand for immediate gratification. Real hope is an ego function, dealing with reality, acknowledging its own needs, yet able to wait for resolution of the situation.[7]

To a large extent the views of hope which were outlined at the beginning of this chapter as characteristic of actual social practice have a pathological basis. In them hope is being presented as dependent on certainty, maintained as long as reality is viewed selectively or symptoms of hopelessness are suppressed. Hope, it is assumed, will automatically remain provided the patient's view of reality is sufficiently circumscribed. If this cannot be achieved successfully, then hope can be delivered as a belief structure to be assented to by the patient, thus avoiding any painful struggle to develop and affirm her own meaning. The latter approach attempts to replace a counterfeit first-order hope with an equally counterfeit second-order hope. Hope has become thoroughly confused with denial.

The view of second- or third-order hope as a belief structure to be applied is similarly hopelessness masquerading as hope. Hope cannot be delivered as a conceptual model, be it Christian or Marxist or anything else, which seeks to evade a personal confrontation with the possibilities inherent within our situation. To really hope we must open ourselves to the pain of false hopes being broken down, the challenge and threat of new possibilities being opened up. We must search within ourselves for the meaning of our own lives, and struggle to reaffirm this meaning in the face of death. The basis for hope is personally-perceived meaning. This meaning may be expressed in, for example, a Christian or an existentialist framework, but giving someone an outline of that framework cannot replace the necessity of that person perceiving meaning in her own existence. Just as pathological first-order hope imposes clarity and demands certainty where clarity and certainty cannot be had without patient waiting, so religious belief can be used to bolster pathological defences, giving ostensible final answers or offering special knowledge which is not linked with ordinary memory and experience.

This of course is not to dismiss the role of religious hope, but merely to caution against certain ways in which religious belief may be misused. To illustrate a religious tendency to want certainty rather than faith and to substitute special knowledge for faithful discipleship,

one has only to look at the strong Gnostic strand which runs through
the history of the church. Here time and again prophet or guru figures
have claimed special knowledge and offered exclusive enlightenment
intended to exempt their followers from ordinary human questions
and struggles. Time and again these movements, which flourish
particularly in times of social uncertainty and unrest, have been
discredited or have proved inadequate to deal with the realities of
human existence.

In outlining the process of hope we have not yet considered
adequately how changes in the nature and content of hope take place.
It is here that the helper's role is vital. But first it might be appropriate
to interpolate a comment about hope and 'telling'.

One of the great debates in the medical literature of terminal care
has been the question of 'telling'; what a patient should be told, and
when, and who should do the telling; whether it is harmful for a dying
person to know his prognosis. I do not wish to enter into this debate
in the terms in which it has been conducted, for this has usually meant
attempting to reach a stereotyped policy which is more likely to suit
doctors than patients. I do, however, want to point out that for hope
to emerge a person needs a realistic assessment of his situation. For
a consultant or family to make a unilateral decision to withhold
information from a dying person is to decide to block that person's
road towards mature hope. The patient may find such a hope through
inferring his prognosis in spite of family or doctor, but it will be a hard
and difficult road. Of course it must also be pointed out that realistic
knowledge does not guarantee hope; realistic knowledge of one's
situation is just as much a part of resignation as it is of affirmation.
Telling is basic to mature hope; but telling alone is not enough. Mere
information cannot create hope.

A further issue in this matter of 'telling' is how in fact the patient
finds out. It needs to be at a time when she is ready to receive and
grapple with the news; which may not be the time the consultant can
most easily fit into his schedule. The point at which a person is ready
to hear depends on a number of factors; personal resources, other
changes which have had to be absorbed, the number and quality of
the supportive relationships the person has. The challenge to the
hospital staff is to find the right time – that is, the patient's time – and
to arrange for the right person to do the telling. This is an aspect of
caring team strategy which we will consider in the penultimate
chapter. It is of course true that there may be some people who will
never be ready to acknowledge or talk about their dying and may need
their defences supported to the last; but the number of such people

would seem to be far smaller than many doctors' policies on telling indicate. There is still a tendency to limit information to all patients on the pretext that a significant proportion will not be able to handle the news. Policies like this in effect deny large numbers of people the opportunity to live and find hope while they are dying.

In turning to consider the helpers' role in the process of hope it seems appropriate to begin with the observation that a strong supportive relationship with another person or persons seems to be common to all cases where there is a hopeful acceptance of death. Sometimes strength and support is drawn from the memory of a past relationship which was central to the person now dying, but there will also be an ongoing relationship in which real care is evident, and where honest disclosure of thoughts and feelings is possible. I think that it is a valid hypothesis to suggest that without such a relationship hope will not emerge, or at least that it is extremely unlikely to emerge.

While dying we may find help in a significant caring relationship with one or several of a number of people. It may be from one of the relationships brought into the dying phase of our life; with marriage partner, children, other relatives, or friends. It may be from a relationship which has its beginning in the dying phase; with a doctor, nurse, social worker, physiotherapist or chaplain. I will for convenience call this partner in the relationship the helper. This is not meant to imply that the helper is in control of change or of the growth of hope. Rather, change is an interpersonal process; the growth of hope is the responsibility of both people in the relationship, but it is under the control of neither. Hope can be shared, not given. It is a quality which emerges within human community.

At the critical point where acceptance of the reality of the situation changes from confusion or even helplessness into hope, nothing changes but perception. The facts remain the same, but the attitude to them is different. The decision to hope cannot be taken on the basis of all the evidence, for the future cannot be predicted with that sort of certainty. The decision to hope must be made when only part of the evidence is available. The strength to make such a decision comes from a trusting, caring relationship. This relationship seems to transcend the evidence, giving a security which replaces any impossible demands for the security of factual certainty. An important factor is the freedom the relationship gives to imagine, to consider possibilities which have not yet appeared. It is a failure of imagination which binds a person to demands for immediate certainty, and causes him to focus exclusively on one part of reality, treating it as if it were the whole and denying the rest.[8]

Fundamentally then the helper offers a relationship within which hope can emerge. The helper cannot guarantee that hope will appear – this is not within her control. If in fact she acts as if she can deliver hope, it is likely that possibilities for hope will be destroyed through the constraints put on the relationship. The helping stance needs to be that discussed earlier in chapter 2 in terms of helplessness and control.

The helper's role initially is that of listener; clarifying, supporting, offering information if this is possible and appropriate. It develops to involve imagining and wishing with the other person; not arguing about the realism of those wishes and hopes, but simply sharing in them. It means encouraging reminiscence, stimulating memory. It may mean offering interpretations, while being sensitive to the fact that questions of meaning come relatively late in the growth of hope, and that early in the dying process what may appear to be questions about meaning (Why me?) are more often expressions of feeling, and should be responded to as such rather than with a theological exposition. A vital part of helping people to hope is the work of clarification and reflection which can enable a dying person to resolve the emotional conflicts dominating the early part of the dying process. Unless this resolution takes place the dying person will not even begin to engage the questions of meaning and purpose which can lead to hope.

Once a realistic perception of his situation is available to a dying person the struggle to hope begins in earnest. At this point the person will need support and perhaps active assistance in uncovering the values and meaning by which he has lived and reassessing these in the light of his new perception. Appropriate assistance includes encouraging the person to remember and to imagine; to go back over his life, telling and reliving the experiences which have shaped his understanding and actions, identifying the people and influences which have formed him as a person. This sort of life review can become personal salvation history, the story of God's acts within his life that makes it possible to look ahead to his death and still wish and imagine possibilities in the face of this apparently impenetrable barrier. The process of life review requires another person to share the journey; and the helper will become actively involved in this process, reviewing her own life, offering some of her own memories and understandings, sharing some of her hopes and fears.

Thus the helping relationship is mutual, with change and hope affecting both participants. The helper will find herself helped and supported, will find her ideas clarified and imagination stimulated, her own memories re-ordered and enriched. Initially perhaps the helper may provide the greater share of the support; but in the end it can often be the 'helper' who is helped by the 'patient'. In caring for dying people we can gain the resources and strength to face our own living and dying.

In Christian ministry the task of remembering and imagining is enriched and encouraged by the resources of faith. Personal salvation history is understood to be linked with the salvation stories of the dying person's community and the whole story of God's redemptive actions in history. Thus an individual's hopes contribute to and are supported by the hopes and wishes of his faith community, and perspective is gained from seeing his life as part of the ongoing life of God's people, specifically within his own community and generally throughout history. Scripture and prayer contribute to this perspective, and communion in particular focusses the process of Christian hope. Here the corporate nature of hope is acknowledged, and past, present and future come together in a dynamic unity. For in the act of communion we remember our history as individuals called to be part of God's people; we are commissioned anew to live as redeemed people in the present day; and we are called towards a new future which will be God's creation. Within the community of faith hope is seen to be directed beyond this world, which is understood to be in transition towards God's future, yet also directed towards the present in that it is concerned with justice, love and service in the world. While for a dying person his opportunity to participate other than vicariously through his community in the pursuit of love and justice is limited, he nevertheless retains the opportunity of witness and service through making a good death, sharing his dying experience for the benefit of others.

To this point our focus has been upon the process through which hope emerges. There has been little comment upon the content of mature hope beyond noting that it is varied and personal, containing hopes about living, hopes about dying, and hopes about death itself. In concluding this chapter it might be interesting to attempt to correlate something of what is being written about hope in contemporary theology with the outline of hope developed here.

Most theologians would see the concept of resurrection to be central to biblical hope, and would make a distinction between this and the traditional doctrine of immortality of the soul.[9] What this distinction might mean in pastoral practice is unfortunately seldom explored. Certainly the effect of focussing upon resurrection has been to restore the balance between past, present and future to theological efforts which had been preoccupied with the past to such an extent that present and future dimensions were neglected. Resurrection emphasizes the shared memory of God's people, places a high value on the necessity and significance of their present strivings, and links these into hope for a future which belongs to God. The emphasis of the theology of hope, as expounded by theologians like Moltmann,[10] has been on community and change; largely this-wordly concerns. And this emphasis has been needed to balance exclusive, pietistic concerns about individual immortality which in effect place Christian hope entirely outside this present world and are hopeless and passive so far as the world is concerned. But with the surge of interest in political theology and liberation theology, associated with the theology of hope, little has been said about the role of personal hope, except in so far as each individual hopes with the rest of the community for God's new future.

Other contemporary movements in theology run parallel with theology of hope, particularly process theology and work based on the thought of Teilhard de Chardin. These approaches share an evolutionary perspective, having their origin in a scientific world view. It is their orientation towards the future which brings them into contact with the theology of hope.[11] The idea of resurrection is much less clear in these evolutionary approaches, but the idea of hope as based on the individual's contribution to the life process is spelled out. The future – and the Being of God – depend upon and incorporate our present action. Death means the end of participation for us, but not the end of our contribution, which continues within the process of Being.[12]

Traditional theologies have given much more attention – sometimes obsessively so – to the individual's hope in the face of death. In practice, however, the conceptual framework and language of this teaching has lost much of its relevance even for practising Christians,[13] and in its pastoral application has become diluted to a comfortable doctrine of immortality. By comfortable I mean that the disruptive character of death is smoothed over, and immortality offered as hope usually without reference to associated doctrines such as judgment.

The theological options available today thus still tend to require an individual to invest his hope on one side or the other of the dividing line of death. Yet the preceding analysis of hope indicates that such a choice is inappropriate. Mature hope contains hopes for both sides of death and is essentially a hope in the person of God, not merely in the value of a personal contribution. Theology still needs to find ways of representing this sort of hope which gives weight both to the value of worldly existence and to a hope for transcendence. This need is recognized by Pannenberg, for example, in his analysis of hope,[14] but it seems that as yet little more than the recognition is forthcoming.[15]

Finally it should be remarked that, leaving aside debate about how the *content* of biblical hope might apply to the contemporary situation, the biblical description of the *process* of hope bears marked parallels with the process outlined above. Certainly in Paul's experience hope is seen as process: 'these sufferings bring patience, as we know, and patience brings perserverance, and perserverance brings hope' (Rom. 5.3b–4). Hope begins in an encounter with the reality of suffering. It involves uncertainty and waiting: 'For we must be content to hope that we shall be saved – our salvation is not in sight, we should not have to be hoping for it if it were – but as I say we must hope to be saved since we are not saved yet – it is something we must wait for with patience' (Rom. 8.24–25). Hope comes as a gift of grace into this situation of patient waiting. It is reinforced by memory, our collective memory of God's saving acts in history, centred in his act of raising Jesus, and also our personal experiences in discipleship. Hope like this springs from making obedience our first priority, obedience which accepts life or death as required, taking on the servant role.[16] A life of discipleship follows a pattern of dying daily,[17] committing aspects of our lives and actions to God who can take these commitments and fashion us into new people. These continuing partial commitments are themselves a rehearsal for dying, where we must take all that we have and are and commit this in trust to God. In one sense then the commitment of everything in our dying is the culmination of our discipleship; and because it extends us far beyond any other commitments we have previously made it is also the greatest test of our faith.

Hope in resurrection expresses well the radical nature of this third-order hope which has been arrived at through struggle and patient waiting, and chosen on the basis of a life committed to particular values and priorities. Resurrection is a hope which does not deny the reality and threat of death, but looks beyond it for an act of God bringing new meaning and possibility. In this sense it stands in contrast to the Greek doctrine of immortality which blurs the transition between life and death and reduces the perceived force of God's initiative. Immortality relies on the idea of the soul, a bit of us which continues automatically through death into eternity. Resurrection begins with a real death, an utter and final commitment of ourselves into the hands of God, who can raise us up. We cannot presume on our worthiness to be raised – but we can trust God as we have found him trustworthy in life.

Thus the prelude to resurrection is our powerlessness, a recognition that we are helpless in the face of death and finitude, and that only God can bring meaning out of this situation. Resurrection begins as hope is given to us, enabling us to live creatively in spite of death; it comes as a new perception given by God's grace. This changed perception both opens out and reinterprets our past, and points us towards an unknown future in which the resurrection hope will take shape. The details of this hope are not known, but they are foreshadowed in Jesus, and validated for us by faith as we accept Jesus' call and commission as disciples. Hope is already with us, and yet it is still to be:

> My dear people, we are already the children of God
> but what we are to be in the future has not yet been revealed,
> all we know is, that when it is revealed
> we shall be like him
> because we shall see him as he really is   (I John 3.2).

5
· *Dying Well* ·

Attempting to envisage an 'appropriate death' may seem at first to be a rather abstract exercise, but it has significant practical importance. Our largely-unarticulated ideas about what an appropriate death might be shape the care we offer dying people and the expectations we have of them. The simple exercise of sitting down and imagining our own dying – where am I? how old am I? who is with me? what do I see, hear, smell, feel. . .? – will quickly put us in touch with some of the hopes, fears, preferences, reluctances about death which influence our behaviour towards others who are dying. It is an exercise worth doing.

This sort of reflection is not, however, a feature of our contemporary society. While other ages appear to have reached a reasonable social consensus on what constitutes an appropriate death, we have not. True, we agree on certain special cases. Some deaths are seen as unfortunate but acceptable because they are the outcome of a sport such as motor-racing or mountain climbing. Some deaths are praise-worthy – soldiers defending their country, firemen rescuing civilians from a blaze. Death at a young age is not acceptable unless in one of the above special categories. Death by accident or trauma is tragic – and newsworthy. To die suddenly, with little or no awareness of dying itself, after at least a few good years of retirement, is generally agreed to be a 'good way to go'. Most of these, however, are extraordinary deaths. We have little to say about how an ordinary person can fashion a good death out of the various possibilities which present themselves in ordinary dying. Unfortunately, neither have those actually involved in terminal care done anything much to redress this situation through exploring the issue with their patients. Thus an appropriate death – in an institution at least – becomes by default as it were one which creates a minimum of fuss or disruption of staff mood and institutional routine.

This is why a 'good death' in a typical medical facility has been described by Robert Kastenbaum[1] as one which adheres to these standards:

1. the good or successful d ath is quiet, uneventful. Nobody is disturbed. The death slips by with as little notice as possible.

2. Not too many people are around. In other words, there is no 'scene'. Staff does not have to adjust to the presence of family and other visitors who have their own needs and who are in various kinds of 'states'.

3. Leave-taking behaviour is at a minimum.

4. The physician does not have to involve himself intimately in terminal care, especially as the end approaches.

5. The staff make few technical errors throughout the entire terminal care process, and few mistakes in 'etiquette'.

6. Strong emphasis is given to the body, little to the personality or spirit of the terminally-ill person in all that is done for or to him.

7. The person dies at the right time: that is, after the full range of medical interventions has been tried, but before a lingering period sets in.

8. The staff are able to conclude that 'we did everything we could for this patient'.

9. The patient expresses gratitude for the excellent care received.

10. After the patient's death the family expresses gratitude for the excellent care provided.

11. Parts or components of the deceased are made available to the hospital for clinical, research or administrative purposes (via autopsy permission or organ donation).

12. A memorial (financial) gift is made to the hospital in the name of the deceased.

13. The cost of the entire terminal care process is determined to be low or moderate; money was not wasted on a person whose life could not be 'saved'.

This description has a polemical flavour reflecting its American origins in a number of places. Nevertheless the material presented in preceding chapters indicates its general validity for Western medicine. The point which Kastenbaum makes in a telling way is that most contemporary medical conceptions of an appropriate death have a great deal to do with the needs of the helpers, but may have little or nothing to do with the needs of the patient and family.

There seems to be a paradox here. Our modern system of medical care had its origins within Judaeo-Christian understandings of life and death,[2] the same understandings which in the past gave ordinary people guidelines for dying as well as living. Yet in the last century our attitudes have changed: once we saw death as having primarily a religious significance; now it is primarily a medical event. Somewhere within this transition we have lost contact with the possibility that death might have a positive meaning for life. It may be helpful to trace the history of our Judaeo-Christian tradition and see how this heritage – religious and medical – shapes our contemporary situation.

The earlier strata of the Old Testament view death as an endpoint, the cessation of life. The dead exist, but they no longer live in any meaningful sense. The grave is their final resting place. In the poetic writings in particular the concept of Sheol as the place of the shades of the departed is found, but this is scarcely more positive. The dead are cut off from Yahweh, who is God of the living: the dead cannot praise him, they cannot hope for his truth.[3] A man is satisfied if he dies in old age at the end of a long happy life. Such a life can be chosen by the man who obeys God's laws, while rejection of the law brings death for disobedience. The choice between the way of life and the way of death thus is open.[4] Alongside these attitudes, however, there are signs of a conflict in understanding which centres on the problem of righteous suffering. In fact many godly men die tragic, early deaths, while many scoundrels flourish, enjoying long and prosperous lives. The idea of the justice of God thus demands a final vindication of the oppressed righteous and punishment for the prosperous oppressor.[5] This conflict is openly stated and agonized over, principally in laments, but no resolution is forthcoming until Israel looks at solutions which go beyond the barrier of death.

It was the Book of Daniel, one of the later writings of the Old Testament period, which first developed in detail an idea of individual survival of death, and this idea became increasingly widespread in Palestinian Judaism after the time of the Maccabees.[6] It was an expectation of a life based not in any innate power of the soul, but created by God through resurrection from the dead. The belief grew out of the experience of righteous suffering of Palestinian Jews during the Seleucid oppression of Palestine. Hellenistic Judaism, already dispersed through the Greek world, only partially adopted the Palestinian concept of resurrection, and the Greek doctrine of immortality was frequently substituted for it.[7]

New Testament attitudes to death grew out of this tradition, which is the framework for much of Jesus' teaching.[8] Jesus, however, does not make death the centre of his message; he calls for repentance and trust in God. He is not interested in speculation concerning details of an after-life.[9] In his discussions he introduces death to point the seriousness of present decisions. He does not use the hope of resurrection to undercut the importance of life. It is our relationship with God which is of primary importance. He refuses to draw any direct inference from the manner of a person's death as to God's verdict on that life. His teaching and his own death reverse the popular assumption that a righteous man can expect a good death.

The New Testament writings continue this emphasis made by Jesus. It is a life of obedience to God which really matters. Resurrection is expected to take place as part of the whole drama of the End, when God will assert himself to rectify or even replace the world. That these times have already started is evident from the resurrection of Jesus, who forms the focus for their hope in God. The work of Christ has destroyed death, and the believer now takes on Christ's death in order to live for the Lord. The believer is 'in Christ' in both life and death.[10] Consequently death is to be confronted hopefully, for now it is seen to be part of God's whole scheme of redemption. The believer must still die, but already the events which will annihilate death and transform life have been set in motion. The impending resurrection gives to life here and now a whole new character.

With the delay of the End or parousia and the impact of Hellenistic thought forms, speculative questions gained a stronger hold on the church's attention. Theologians made attempts to reconcile diverse New Testament perspectives on death, and increasingly brought them into dialogue with Greek culture, in which the immortality of the soul was axiomatic. Among the early Fathers a number of different solutions to the question of the after-life are to be seen, and with each is associated a particular view of an appropriate death. Tatian, for example, declares war on the Greek concepts of immortality and pre-existence. He emphasizes God's absolute sovereignty; his power to create man and re-create him if needs be. Tatian is evidently concerned to oppose a doctrine of natural immortality which he fears will lead to hope becoming separated from God's action in Christ. He sees the core of Christian belief to be pessimism about life, but optimism about God. Death is good because it delivers man from a life of deterioration and sin. It is a release to be welcomed; what lies beyond however is in the hands of God, and little can be said about it.[11]

Tatian's rejection of Greek metaphysics is, however, atypical for his time. Clement of Alexandria affirms the Platonic idea of immortality, and accepts in a qualified form the idea of the pre-existence of the soul. Death becomes in his understanding a liberation, something to be faced with calm detachment, without the existential pathos which characterizes Tatian's view.[12] Cyprian represents yet another perspective, a form of Christian stoicism. The Christian, like all men, suffers and dies. He too has the trials and consolations of a natural man. Death is thus a rest from the sorrow and labour of life. It is to be endured; but with hope in Christ who has overcome death.[13]

These and other similar perspectives emerged from the dialogue between Christian tradition and Greek philosophy. From each came a view of an appropriate death, whether it be the calm and joyful death of Clement or the stoical death of Tatian or Cyprian. But the overall effect of this sort of thinking was that concern for the plight of the soul after death and fear concerning its destiny began to dominate Christian reflection on death. Increasingly, theologians became unwilling to endure unanswered questions, and as a result the highly-developed Greek metaphysics of immortality overwhelmed resurrection concepts which had no such developed metaphysics associated with them. Correspondingly the focus of interest came increasingly upon individual salvation, with the resurrection emphasis on God's corporate salvation and restoration of his people being lost.[14]

By the early Middle Ages a relatively consistent doctrine of after-life was established, with the soul being understood to experience a period of waiting between death and the Final Judgment. The balance sheet of each life was not closed at death, but at the end of time. Thus personal biography continued beyond physical death and decay,[15] giving the living opportunity to exert an influence through prayers and offerings upon the eternal destiny of those who had died. During the Middle Ages themselves the character of the period between death and final judgment altered. Judgment was in effect transferred to the time of death, and the doctrine of Purgatory developed, a doctrine which in the late Middle Ages culminated in the gross exploitation of indulgences.

In mediaeval times, then, physical death was increasingly the focus for attention, exerting a fearful fascination over the whole culture.[16] This preoccupation with the details of death and judgment led in turn to an increasingly specific view of appropriate death. Dying people were now seen as the centre of a cosmic struggle for their souls, a struggle which produced the 'greatest and most grievous temptation, and such as they had never had before in all their life'.[17] Details of the correct approach to death were specified, with appropriate ritual actions laid down for all concerned. The family and relatives attended the death, and farewells were said, the dying person himself presiding over the ritual. Should he lapse from it, it was the responsibility of those present to recall him to it.[18] The art of dying was general knowledge, religious in character, but by no means dominated by the clergy. Only confession and absolution were specifically ecclesiastical, and even these could be performed by a layman should the need arise. Dying was thus a public demonstration. The manner of dying revealed to the onlookers the probable verdict which was to come at the Final Judgment; a good death was very important. There was also the aspect of a last test; woodcuts from the late Middle Ages depict God and his court observing the dying man during his trial – a trial which will determine his fate in eternity. At the point of death the dying man reviewed his whole life and saw its meaning. His attitude at that moment could erase all his sins should he ward off temptation, or cancel all his good deeds if he gave way. Dying contained 'the security of a collective rite, and the anxiety of a personal interrogation'.[19] The moment of death had been made of absolute importance.

With the Reformation came a disruption of this established view of mortality. The destruction of the doctrine of Purgatory and the weakening of certainty regarding details of the after-life released people from their macabre preoccupation with physical decay, although it must be said that some Protestant scholars quickly built a doctrine of predestined damnation which could be as terrifying as any of the mediaeval excesses. Nevertheless, Reformation understandings on the whole enabled a more balanced perspective to be held, with due appreciation of the relationship between godly living and eternal destiny.

For Luther the Christian's death is supported by assurance: the believer can trust in God's love. Experiences of suffering and death are painful, but they have an inner meaning. Through sickness and weakness the believer is driven to rely upon the grace of God which in this world still appears as it did in Christ; through obedient suffering. Christian suffering thus can become an identification with Christ so that death, despite all outward appearances, is 'harmless enough and puts an end to sins and vices'.[20] A similar attitude to death is held by Calvin. Death is both agony and blessing. It requires from the dying person stoical endurance, and yet witnesses to the grace which reconciles man and God. The dying person can be seen to increase in spiritual strength towards the end, and in the act of dying may make truest witness to his friends. As death draws near, his friends and family pray with him and exhort him, but the dying person also ministers to them. In the act of dying he can verify that reconciliation with God is a reality which enables death to be faced with confidence. Death is a moment which shows the truth about the

individual, and can also show the truth of our human condition; that
God's grace is paramount.[21]

Stress on the significance of a dying person's conduct and on the
circumstances of his death thus continued beyond the Middle Ages.
Differing emphases, however, emerged from different traditions. The
Counter Reformation found spiritual writers struggling against the
popular belief that there was little point in virtuous living as a good
death could redeem a lifetime of vice.[22] The seventeenth century also
saw a variety of views ranging from those of the Anglican divine
Jeremy Taylor who saw death as 'so harmless a thing, that no good
man was ever thought the more miserable for dying, but much the
happier',[23] to the New England Puritans whose doctrine of necessary
doubt of salvation made death a time of final trial and struggle.

Taylor's work *Holy Living and Dying* was written as an aid to
Church of England people without pastoral oversight during the
Commonwealth. Unlike the mediaeval art of dying literature it was
intended for use by people in full health in order to prepare them for
inevitable sickness and death. It is a book which specifies attitudes,
preparations and actions concerning sickness and dying. Its picture
of an appropriate death is one which is prepared for by a virtuous life,
a final sickness which is accepted as an opportunity for spiritual
growth, and a death bereft of fear and doubt through repose in God.
In contrast to mediaeval attitudes, Taylor saw death-bed repentance
as unlikely and probably inadequate.[24] His view of the obstacles
encountered in preparation for death was realistic, and he dealt fully
with the trials and temptations of sickness, including the fear of death
and despair. He gave also a detailed outline for pastoral care of the
dying person, taking pains in warning against any assumptions
concerning the dying person's true spiritual status based only on
observation of the moment of dying.[25]

The Puritans who removed themselves to New England in reaction
to the re-established Anglican tradition in England after the Commonwealth developed a very different attitude to death.[26] While they
maintained traditional Christian rhetoric concerning death as the
release of the soul, they were in fact gripped by an unremitting fear of
death, resulting from the form of their doctrine of grace. Stannard
describes their dilemma in this way:

> Their theology taught them of their utter and total depravity, of
> their helplessness in securing their own salvation, and reinforced
> this pessimism with the doctrine of assurance; doubt of salvation
> was essential to salvation and that Puritan who, for so long as he

breathed, became at any time secure and comfortable in the knowledge of his salvation, was surely lost.[27]

This is the reverse of the mediaeval view of an appropriate death. In the later Middle Ages a dying person was held to attain salvation through resolutely clinging to an optimistic belief in his own goodness and the justice of God. In New England, what had been assurance for the dying person of mediaeval Europe was seen as the terrible temptation of the dying Puritan. He was tempted to rest in an assurance of salvation based on his good works – and he found salvation through denying this. Such agonizing conflict could not long be endured. The latter half of the eighteenth century saw the disappearance of this doctrine of necessary doubt, and a renewed focus upon the idea of an exemplary Christian death stressing the element of witness we have already seen in Calvin. In the early nineteenth century this idea seems to dominate the evangelical tradition at least. The Christian's death was a distinctive witness, a form of verification of the claims of the Gospel. William Ward, in a published address to 'the Hindoos' could say; 'Oh, dear Hindoos, you never saw a true Christian die. Instead of fearing death, he desires to be absent from the body, and present with the Lord: for him to die is gain.'[28] Such descriptions of Christian death as verification were common, but the form outlasted the substance. Reports of death-bed scenes and last words of the deceased became more and more stereotyped until finally and fairly abruptly they disappeared altogether from the Christian journals in the latter half of the nineteenth century. Death ceased to be a pubic event.

These changes coincided with the rise of clinical medicine which dates its beginning from the late eighteenth century. Medicine changed its orientation from an art based on discourse with the patient to a science based on observation of the patient. The new focus on systematic observation and classification laid the foundation for diagnostic and prognostic medicine in much the form that we experience it today. That these decades at the end of the eighteenth and beginning of the nineteenth centuries produced fundamental changes in medical and social consciousness is persuasively argued by Foucault.[29]

A fundamental part of this new consciousness was a changed attitude to death. Previously death had stood as a barrier to medical knowledge, removing the patient from any further discourse with the doctor. Now for the pathological anatomists death became a key to illuminate life and disease:

> For twenty years, from morning to night, you have taken notes at the patients' bedsides on affections of the heart, the lungs and the gastric viscera, and all is confusion for you in the symptoms which, refusing to yield up their meaning, offer you a succession of incoherent phenomena. Open up a few corpses: you will dissipate at once the darkness that observation alone could not dissipate.[30]

This new clinical perspective, in its desire to understand symptoms and distinguish the general patterns of disease processes, began to focus more upon diagnosis and treatment than upon the patient. The resultant depersonalizing of medical practice quite early became a concern to some doctors. Carl Friedrich Marx in his work on care of the dying in 1826 emphasized the doctor's responsibility to avoid dubious therapeutic measures and to concentrate on appropriate palliative treatment. He drew attention to the doctor's opportunity for pastoral care – the 'administering of some kind of higher comfort' – which should not be left to the priest, for in doing so the doctor deprives himself of 'the most noble and rewarding aspect of his work'.[31] Nevertheless, the new medical consciousness slowly and inexorably had its effect upon social perceptions and behaviours concerning death. Phillipe Aries charts this change of social consciousness through a description of dying in nineteenth-century literature.[32] He shows how advances in diagnostic medicine allowed earlier and more accurate prognoses for illness, and with it bestowed upon the physician a power to forecast life or death; how in turn a natural reluctance to give patients the status of being 'marked for death' led to physicians withholding information from patients and requiring families to live a lie; how death changed from being a public to a private event, because it is not easy to reverse at the last the patterns of the lie that has been lived; how with increasing medicalization the location of death changes from home to hospital. In the space of a few generations, in the Western world at least, dying and death changed from being understood primarily in religious terms to being seen primarily as medical concerns.

Current religious attitudes towards death seem to be a curious mixture of fragments of their historical precursors and our contemporary denial or isolation of death. There are within the church some remnants of the concept of a distinctively Christian death, but there is little expectation that this will characterize the deaths of all Christians. Some traditions retain rituals for the dying, but again these are no longer universally employed, and seldom involve the dying person as central actor in the drama of dying. (Prayers for the dying are typically said over an unconscious patient, for example.) Tentativeness concerning pastoral ministry to dying people is evident in practice, and in 'pastoral' advice which defers almost completely to clinical perspectives on terminal care management.[33] Generally speaking there is no expectation that the death of Christians will bear witness. No prescriptive mode of dying is taught in religious circles; although interestingly there are examples of a new secular art of dying literature,[34] while recent biographical accounts of the dying of well-known Christian leaders may in time lead to a revised Christian understanding of a 'good death'.[35] But today death is no longer a public act; frequently a person dies alone, and certainly children are rarely allowed to be present at a death-bed, as they were in earlier times. The church's attitudes today seem drawn from current social beliefs rather than from pastoral tradition. The religious framework has incorporated denial of death, making religious ministry to dying people a difficult and often ambiguous affair. Salvation has been presented as a way to avoid death rather than as a way which enables us, among other things, to make a good death; suffering has been interpreted as judgment rather than seen as part of life and a means of growth; the doctrine of immortality has been used to trivialize physical death – it is not surprising that there is not much to say to people who are in the final weeks of life.

This fragmentation is reflected in the cursory attention given death in most contemporary theological writing. Even those theologians who do focus on death seem to have little concern or interest in the pastoral strategies which might issue from their work. Examples from two quite different theological streams serve to illustrate this.

Final option theory is a view associated principally with the Catholic theologians Boros[36] and Troisfontaines.[37] They see the moment of death presenting a man with his first completely free personal act. While living, he has been able only to progress towards freedom; now in death he has a final option for which life itself has been a rehearsal. At death he sees God, the world, and himself in full reality, and makes a completely free and irrevocable choice between communion with God and isolation from God.

The work of both Boros and Troisfontaines strikes me as an intricate exercise in speculative theology, motivated principally by doctrinal interests. Final option theory has been applied to clarify and interpret a number of doctrines, such as those concerning limbo, purgatory, and salvation of the unbaptized. Applications to pastoral strategies in terminal care are less easy to uncover, nor is there any adequate discussion of the ways in which our encounters with mortality and finitude in this life might shape our personalities and thus our living and dying. It is difficult to escape the conclusion that final option theory devalues discipleship, and hence pastoral care. If the final decision is to be completely free, it must be completely dissociated from the life which precedes it, despite the proponents' claims that a virtuous life will aid the final decision. The pastor may sense a mystery unfolding in the dying person, to use Boros' words, but what the pastor can offer in this situation is not stated. The dying person appears to be left with the knowledge of an imminent final test for which he cannot really prepare.

While final option theory draws strongly from the mediaeval tradition, albeit recast within an existentialist framework, process theology is a movement based on the philosophy of Alfred North Whitehead.[38] A process theologian like Hartshorne[39] sees dying as the completion of a life which will remain forever within the memory of God. The person's actions for good or ill are preserved. Death may be tragic, if a person's potential has been wasted or his life cut off before fruition; or appropriate, if a person has participated in life in such a way that he has given all he has to give. What remains to a person while dying is a memory of his contribution, and the hope that it will prove to be of lasting significance in the cosmic process. Again, little is written concerning the implications of this perspective for terminal care. It would seem that a pastor's role is that of reassurance, reminding the person that the contribution of his or her life will never be forgotten by God; and support, offered out of respect for what the person has been and has given. While this stance offers somewhat more pastoral direction than final option theory, it still has little to say to the transcendent aspects of a dying person's hopes.

With little offered by contemporary theological thought, actual pastoral approaches in terminal illness tend to draw their content from fragments of the tradition; pastoral rituals and the giving of assurance regarding immortality (the related matter of judgment being neglected in most cases). The absence of any clear perception of an appropriate death means, however, that the actual strategies or dynamics of that pastoral care are remarkably like those of other professions, particularly in institutional situations. The implicit values of the institution tend to shape all forms of care offered within it.

Lambourne has argued that the modern hospital has become the 'temple of the twentieth century'; the place which both reflects and shapes our morals.[40] This statement certainly appears to be true of our attitudes to death, and the views of appropriate death implicit within them. The majority of such views, however, are views by default; they are implied through the denial of death. Death is seen as a totally negative event, failure for the doctor and extinction for the patient. Such an attitude may be summarized as 'Death is the worst thing that can happen to a man'.[41] The actions springing from such an attitude have been described in chapter 1, particularly in the discussion of closed and suspicion awareness contexts. Staying alive is the most important thing, so that an appropriate death is impossible by definition. And the definition is bound to persist. Those who hold to it will not create the conditions for any other sort of death.

A model of appropriate death exists among advocates of euthanasia, in the sense now of 'the painless inducement of death'.[42] An appropriate death is chosen by the dying person, who can elect to escape from the pain and stress of dying by requesting a medical staff member to hasten his end. While control is ostensibly in the hands of the dying person, legislation to prevent that control from passing into the hands of family members or staff (or the state) has proved almost impossible to frame. A strong current of opinion suggests that general improvement in terminal care, along the lines of that already given in hospices, should remove many of the present grounds for advocating euthanasia.[43]

Weisman suggests a number of criteria which could be taken to define an appropriate death:

> Someone who dies an appropriate death must be helped in the following ways: he should be relatively pain-free, his suffering reduced, and emotional and social impoverishment kept to a minimum. Within the limits of disability, he should operate on as high and effective a level as possible, even though only tokens of former fulfilments can be offered. He should also recognize and resolve residual conflicts, and satisfy whatever remaining wishes are consistent with his present plight and his ego ideal. Finally, among his choices, he should be able to yield control to others in whom he has confidence. He also has the option of seeking or relinquishing significant key people.[44]

Weisman acknowledges the idealistic nature of this description, but points out that our present perception that death is never appropriate may well be a self-fulfilling idea. Better, he argues, to attempt at least to help a dying person to achieve the sort of death he might choose for himself – if he had a choice.

The ideal which Weisman is talking of has been called 'death with dignity', a term which describes the situation when a person is still able to see himself as a worthwhile individual while dying. In this perspective it is the patient who determines what is appropriate. Death with dignity is possible (although by no means guaranteed) when a dying individual is surrounded by people who give him loving and respectful attention. Under these circumstances dying can bring about further personal development.[45]

I would concur with Weisman that good terminal care should offer the support and possibilities he has indicated. I am not so sure that fulfilment of these criteria enables us to call the death appropriate even though, as Weisman remarks, an appropriate death may depart markedly from an 'ideal' death.[46] It seems to me that some deaths may be appropriate even though they do not meet the Weisman criteria. For example, there are individuals who will insist upon maintaining denial right to the end; others will fight – literally – until their last breath. Neither approach is very satisfactory; but it may be thoroughly appropriate to the dying person's life. And for me to say that it is not satisfactory of course reveals something of what I think dying ought to be like. But should I as a carer place my expectations on a dying person?

This latter question is at the core of the question of an appropriate death, and has not been answered adequately by proponents of 'death with dignity'. In some manifestations, in America in particular, this movement has adopted a facile optimism with regard to dying and death; death is beautiful, natural, and can be welcomed as a friend; dying is simply an opportunity to grow. To hold up values and expectations like this before some dying people is just as oppressive and unhelpful as the 'conspiracy of silence' approach which we have already criticized.[47] Rather, the criteria for an appropriate death must be acceptable to the dying person. Often these criteria will not be ones which the caring team regard as ideal. Professional carers need to know their patients and themselves well enough to judge which criteria should be accepted without further question, which should be negotiated further, and which supportively confronted. The variety of perceptions of appropriate death also has implications for our structures of care. There is little point in making, for example, hospice care the only model of terminal care available to all if this approach will be anathema to some dying people.

In a society which removes death from everyday life in the way we do, it may be that all we can aim for is to allow people to die appropriately, making their deaths as consistent with their lives as circumstances permit. To go beyond this requires us as a society to make death more central in our thinking and experience, rather than avoid the fact of our finitude to the extent we now do. This in turn may require us to reclaim some of the neglected elements of our tradition: an idea of a good death; and a way of participating in the death of others so that we can learn from them – so that each person's death has some public character, witnessing to the values of their life. In a way this movement has already begun with the proliferation of accounts by and about dying people published in recent years. In these we see emphasized for the most part the possibilities of the human spirit faced with finitude and death. Perhaps we also need to have more accounts of deaths which demonstrate the paucity and inadequacy of the lives they complete. We need the first sort of story so that we can be hopeful about our dying; and the second sort so that we do not naively assume that a good death comes naturally. In fact, as we all know, there is nothing automatic about a good death. Those who find it do so through struggle, often having to claim the death they want in the face of constraints placed upon them by society, professional helpers and friends.

I have just used the term 'a good death', which is clearly a value-laden concept. I use it in a way similar to the way I have used appropriate death. An appropriate death is one consistent with the life it brings to a close. Similarly, from my perspective, a good death is one which ends a good life; a life which gives us something to remember, to cherish, to carry forward, to hope for. This death may well be early, sudden or tragic, but even the suddenness or tragic nature of our loss can draw us together in our suffering and break open new possibilities through shared grief and mutual support. As I write this I have before me in my mind's eye several faces – the faces of people whose untimely deaths were body-blows to the church community of which I am a member, yet whose loss gathered us and formed us as a community in a new way. To say this is in no way intended to diminish the loss and pain experienced by their families and indeed by us all, but simply to point out that even from these tragic, premature deaths of good people came new life and fresh hope for their community.

I believe that it is important that we assess a death in terms of the life it ends and the legacy left behind, rather than by focussing on the nature of the death itself. We need to do this lest we fall into the error of judging a person's life by the death they have died. And we must avoid this error in order to live authentically. None of us can assume that his or her death will be appropriate – the circumstances of death are so often beyond our control. But we can ensure that our death will be a good death in terms of the commitments we make and the directions we choose in our living.

Central to my concept of a good death is an understanding of Christian community. A good death takes place within a community where people are known and cherished and valued for who they are as well as the contribution they make – where indeed their primary contribution to community may be who they are rather than anything in particular they do. In such a community each death creates a painful gap and changes the community. Yet out of the mutual support and shared grief new contributions to corporate life emerge, meaning is slowly and painfully uncovered even for inappropriate deaths, and growth continues.

Community is essential both to absorb the suffering and realize the legacy left through the death of a good person. For a community to be able to do this, it must have certain characteristics. For a start, it must affirm the importance of an open awareness of death, and practice this in its corporate life. This is of course an emphasis common to Old and New Testaments: an awareness of our finitude is a prerequisite for wisdom, authentic living.[48] If we are aware that we must die, we can no longer commit ourselves with confidence to our possessions or to fostering illusions about ourselves. We will need to look for meaning elsewhere – in God. The Biblical message is that there is no way past death, but God has given us his Spirit as a pledge of the hope that on the other side of death he is still Lord, and that he will not allow his story with us to be broken off. Such a hope assumes that there is a story relating us with God this side of death, and again this brings us to community. The Spirit who is God's agent of hope gathers and empowers and continues to create community. Our story with God is the story of our participation in his community, and our experience in community is the basis of our hope. As we enter community, commit ourselves to hear and respond to God's call, share our lives with others that we might come to a realistic assessment of ourselves, and engage in interdependent ministry, so we discover who we are to be and what we are to do.[49]

Thus a good death requires a community which encourages and nurtures the journey of faith from hearing God's call through to exercising that call in ministry. Such a community must be open to receiving and valuing new people; it must be direct and essentially affirmative in its communication; it must be prepared to test, recognize and accommodate the variety of personal contributions which emerge within its life, not overvaluing some and diminishing others. In short it must be a truly interdependent community where people are vulnerable to each other and to the world, a place where people are recognized and affirmed in their contribution while they are living, not merely after they have died. When death takes a member of a community like this that person's death is a witness, because the entire community is changed through losing them, and because God continues to create new life through faithful suffering and hoping.

I have written this in terms of Christian community. I recognize that other people may wish to pursue other forms of community; and I recognize that the local church is seldom the sort of community it should be in the light of the Gospel. Nevertheless, I maintain that we need community to cope with and reach some sort of understanding of death, and that this community needs to be one in which people are known and valued by each other, sharing a common purpose which transcends the lives of the individuals involved. If I am right in this, it must have profound implications for urban societies in which this sort of community has broken down almost completely. And it raises questions about our current models of professional care which do not attempt to create or co-operate with community, even in some cases not attempting to know the person who is the object of care. We will deal further with these issues in the final chapter.

6

· *Better Terminal Care* ·

Preceding chapters have offered a critique of our present methods of terminal care, identifying some major inadequacies and also suggesting approaches which may lead to improvements. Here we gather these suggestions together and explore some implications for the way care is structured in our society. The focus will still be on terminal care, but the implications will lead us to a general reappraisal of institutional care and the professional structures which sustain it.

Helping

Central to this book is an understanding of the helping role which is grounded in a pastoral perspective although, as I trust I have demonstrated, it is derivable from and supported by insights from other disciplines as well. Key characteristics are that care should be person centred and wholistic, not confining itself to any single aspect of need but willing to recognize and work with the interpenetrating physical, social, emotional and spiritual components of an individual's need. This care is offered within a mutual relationship, in which a professional person's power (knowledge and skill) is used co-operatively, not coercively. Mutuality also characterizes the relationships between the various professional people involved in the provision of care. Thus helping relationships are genuinely open human relationships in which new understanding can emerge, responsibility can be shared, and people can change. This learning, sharing and change will affect both participants in a relationship. Openness to change also involves risk, as we have seen. A mutual relationship makes a helper vulnerable to the tragic dimension of human existence, present especially when the helping relationship is with a dying person and family.

Using professional knowledge and skills creatively within mutual relationships adds a further dimension to a helping professional's development and practice. The acquisition and application of know-ledge and skills alone is not enough; the professional must have a personal and vocational identity secure enough to be exposed on a continuing basis to the challenge and risk of mutual relationship. Such identity does not form automatically as knowledge and skills are acquired; its formation and nurture should be intentional, incorpor-ated into professional training and practice. I would further assert that in fact such identity can only be adequately formed in community – both the community of professionals and the wider human community.

This understanding of the helping role began with reflection upon a fundamental problem in institutional terminal care; the fact that depression and resignation may be precipitated and reinforced by the structures of the institution itself. Our analysis indicated that a change in institutional structure requires a corresponding change in institutional roles, which in turn means a revised understanding of professionalism. We begin to examine practical implications of this helping stance by considering these factors as they arise within team work in terminal care.

Team work in terminal care

Chapter 1 concluded with three guidelines for terminal care, one of which was the need for multi-disciplinary approaches to care. Recently it has become fashionable to label such approaches team work. I suspect however that many so-called teams are scarcely multi-disciplinary in fact, being dominated by just one or two perspectives, and that some of them compound the patients' problems by offering them organized paternalism rather than mutual relationships with team members. If we are to speak of team work we will need to become rather more explicit about the composition and method of operation of the team.

The purpose of a multi-disciplinary team is to offer wholistic care; to be equipped to respond to all aspects of the broad spectrum of needs experienced, in our case, in the dying situation. Thus the team needs to be able to respond to physical, emotional, social and spiritual issues, and to do so co-operatively, recognizing that presenting issues are seldom limited to any one of the four-fold categories mentioned above. The breadth of response required raises questions about the composition of the team. Ideally there should be input from all those who have a significant contribution to or participation in the dying situation. This would clearly include the patient, his family and friends, and a range of community support people. It would also include a whole variety of people involved in institutional care. Again ideally, some of those from the institution might well be people who are not usually involved in case conferences – the cleaners and ward clerks, for example, who often have unique and valuable insights into the patients' situations. Practically of course such a team would be unwieldy in the extreme – simply convening a meeting would be a major undertaking. And so one of the fundamental decisions of team work is about who will be included in the team and who will be left out. This is a decision which should be made carefully, not just along the lines of precedent or by rules such as professionals in, lay people and volunteers out. A great deal of team work is nullified or diminished in value because it has no access to areas of life which are of real significance to the patient; and of course those areas often, indeed usually, are outside the scope of the institution. Even when certain people are excluded from the team – and for logistical reasons it will usually be most of those outside the institution – it is important that there be a process by which they can contribute to team considerations (through a designated liason person, for example), and that they are aware of that process.

However, while there are logistical problems with a team approach (and other problem areas which we will address shortly), the advantages of team care in terminal illness are clear. A team approach enables a whole spectrum of needs to be met. Proper team communication ensures that each person involved in care has an overview of the situation and is not limited to an individual disciplinary perspective. Team functioning also allows for a pooling of insights and information which can be extremely important in building this overview. What may appear to be odd comments or random behaviour from a patient can take on a new significance as a pattern emerges in the team meeting; as for example with a time-disoriented patient who may make a series of connected statements over a period of hours, but address each of them to a different person. Similarly, team functioning gives some answer to the way in which many patients will discuss social problems with the nurses, spiritual issues with the doctor, medical problems with the social worker and their bowels with the chaplain. At least in the team meeting the right information can get to the right people! A further important strength of the team approach is the support available to team members from one another, and the sense of sharing responsibility rather than having to bear it alone. Of course this sense of solidarity can be abused if, for example, it enables staff to assume a united front in controlling the patient. The risk of this happening is significantly increased if the patient and family are not given access to team decision making.

Breadth of response, improvement in communication, and personal support for carers are thus three aspects significantly improved by a team approach. Ensuring that these are used to care for rather than control patients establishes further requirements for the team. Basically the team needs to be composed of people committed to mutual relationships with one another, and able to offer the same quality of relationship in care. For professional members of the team this requirement in itself runs counter to a great deal of the professional behaviour which seems to be concerned with establishing territory and defending it against other disciplines. Mutuality here implies a willingness to commit ourselves to other people, and maintain this commitment as we work through the problems of different language and differing perspectives which are inherent in any interdisciplinary dialogue. Only with this level of personal commitment can a team be maintained and learn to work co-operatively, gaining enough understanding of one another's disciplines so that each can distinguish the signs which will be of significance to others, even if they have no direct relevance to his or her professional practice. Also implied by the requirement of mutuality is the need for a team to be self-conscious about its corporate life. Time needs to be spent in learning to be a team and in reflecting on team practice. Task orientation is not enough.

A real obstacle to successful team formation is the level of personal commitment required. For professionals trained in an institutional context this means changing their expectations of working relationships. Institutions operate with a functional view of staff: doctors are doctors; one doctor is (within reason) as good as another; as long as a doctor (any doctor) of the required level of experience is in attendance on each ward then all is well. Teams, however, cannot be assigned on this basis. A team is made up of particular people who share among them a variety of professional skills. A team cannot function as a team if membership is continually changing. This requirement of personal commitment thus has two aspects to it: a team needs to learn to operate as a community; and it may have to operate in tension with its organizational context, particularly if it exists within an institution like a large acute-care hospital.

Many of the difficulties experienced by a team in the process of formation are the sort of difficulties encountered by any diverse group which comes together to undertake a common task. For a team to realize the sort of qualities I have outlined above it needs to be a community; by which I mean an intermediate group which is neither an intimate primary group (like a family) nor an impersonal organization (like a large institution) but which has elements of both.[1] A community requires its members to interact as people, not just as professional functionaries; but it also exists for a specific purpose which is served best by co-operative use of the members' various skills. A terminal care team will have to deal with a number of 'small group' issues as well as with the 'institutional' issues of professional co-operation. The former category includes issues raised by the fact that some professions are predominantly represented by men (doctors, chaplains) and some by women (nurses, social workers); that there is frequently a generation gap between senior consultants and young professionals; that different people have different expectations concerning decision making and other group processes. These differences in sex, age, expectation and personality will need to be confronted as openly and creatively as possible. Otherwise they are likely to appear as institutional issues, translated into demarcation disputes and interdepartmental rivalry.[2]

If a team is to avoid this path, yet still become a genuine team, it will need to give careful and explicit attention to its aims and purpose, its process of decision making, and its mode of leadership. It will also need to carry out regular reviews of its method of operation. In one way for a team to function properly it matters less what actually is decided than that whatever is decided is discussed and agreed upon by the whole team. However, alternative modes of working as a team do need to be considered carefully. With leadership, for example, a *laissez-faire* approach might seem to be appropriate in that it allows different team members to take the lead at times when their expertise is most relevant. This has obvious advantages; but there are also disadvantages with this approach. One is that lines of accountability are blurred, so that communication within the team and liason outside the team can suffer. On the other hand, selecting one person as team leader (in practice usually a doctor) clarifies accountability but may lead to a single disciplinary perspective dominating the team. In other words, there is no ideal system; the team needs to negotiate its own solution, endeavouring of course to compensate for the difficulties created thereby.

All this discussion has tended to lose sight of an earlier comment that ideally patient and family should have a presence on the team or at least participate in its decision-making processes. M. de Wachter claims that in fact inclusion of the patient or client is an important factor in ensuring that a team keeps its focus clear, that interdisciplinary communication is enhanced, and that the team does not abuse its power.[3] He suggests that a team process should have these characteristics: 1. the patient and his request should be received and acknowledged in its human dimension, that is, beyond being 'a case'; 2. all members should be willing to clarify their own motivations and reasons and be equally willing to listen to others without prejudice; 3. responsibility is to be shared by all alike; 4. a follow up of patients should be guaranteed even to those whose request has not be granted; 5. the team must not work secretly but in the open, with its own professional and social identity.[4]

The third point of shared responsibility is emphasized by de Wachter, who sees it as an important indicator of successful team work. Decisions need to be arrived at by corporate process and owned by all members of the team, particularly afterwards when consequences must be faced. To achieve this all the members must be prepared to commit time and energy to the team process; all need to have equal voting rights, so that no individual's participation can be ignored and no one finds himself the mere executor of others' decisions; and the team must have an expectant attitude, believing (hopefully on the basis of prior experience) that resolution will emerge through faithful commitment to the team process. The tendency to rush a team decision must be resisted, especially in situations where an outside specialist is involved, as this person will often bring into the team situation a tendency to reach immediate final conclusions on the basis of partial insights.

The context from which de Wachter writes is five years experience on an interdisciplinary team working with problems in fertility and sterility. Clearly the potential for patient participation in such a team differs from that in the terminal care situation. Because clients are essentially voluntary and are fully active socially, and because it works in such an ethically-sensitive area, the fertility clinic team is very aware of issues of patient control and public accountability. In terminal care the patients' situations may make face to face participation in the team process less feasible. If this is the case it is important to have some sort of patient representative as a functioning member of the team, perhaps a family member or close friend of the patient. This representation will aid the business of clear communication between disciplines, and introduce an element of public accountability to the team process. Without it the team will more easily be seduced into assuming power over the patient, replacing existing caregivers and effectively isolating the patient from continuing social support.

Team members support for each other also needs careful attention in the terminal care unit. It is possible for staff members to avoid personal needs and issues by focussing on the tasks before them and centring their discussions solely on the needs of the patients. While many institutions provide personal support services for staff 'when they are needed', by the time the need is evident and admitted it is often far too late for creative resolution of the problem. It seems preferable to structure some regular group time in which the team focusses on the experiences of its members rather than on the patients. Hopefully this would legitimate supportive sharing among team members, and make it more likely that personal issues are dealt with quickly and effectively before they become personal crises. It would be helpful if such group sessions could be led by a trained supervisor from outside the immediate team.[5]

The internal life of the team needs careful attention. So does the context in which the team operates, for this may place a number of constraints upon team function. For example, if the team is effectively the whole staff of a small institution, then external constraints are few; team work is the primary organizing structure for the institution, and there is considerable freedom in deciding just how the team will operate. It is comparatively easy to offer patient-centred care, and staff members naturally relate at a personal level. If, however, the team is based within a large general hospital the external constraints are multiplied. There will be problems with incompatible organizational structures, with competing demands on team members' time, with different recording systems, with architecture and location within the hospital. The values and methods of a team approach to care will co-exist rather uneasily with many of the administrative and organizational processes of a large hospital; although a team which is clear about its purpose and function will probably be able to claim a place precisely because many of the other units of the hospital are not very clear about their detailed mode of operation. There will be scheduling difficulties when team members have a variety of professional commitments outside the team, and probably the associated difficulty that they will need to change their mind-set each time they return to the team situation from participating in other structures. All this tends to be compounded by practical physical difficulties. Some members of the team will be ward-based, some will work out of departments located elsewhere in the hospital, others again will have only a visiting presence at the hospital. If the team belongs to a specialist unit its patients may be scattered throughout the hospital rather than in the one ward location. And of course most large hospitals lack suitable meeting rooms in ward areas. Under such conditions it is very difficult to develop any sense of corporate identity. Add to this the tendency of large institutions to polarize rather than blur disciplinary distinctions, to require different recording systems for different professions, and to lose their focus on patient care because of a plethora of other educational, research, planning or pecuniary concerns, and it is easy to see why it is difficult for team care to flourish in large institutions. Most true interdisciplinary team work is still associated with specialist units, and in large institutions what passes for team work often gives rise to the reservations about the approach with which this section began.

The appropriateness of multi-disciplinary team work is still unde-cided in health care circles, being part of a continuing debate about ways of optimizing quality of patient care, costs, institutional size and community health needs.[6] In the terminal care field this issue is focussed further as we look at the recent impact of hospice care and the question of its continuing role within contemporary terminal care.

Hospice as an alternative model of care

The hospice has a long history in Christian tradition as a place of welcome, offering hospitality to travellers, especially to those who journey with a burden: the poor, the sick, the dying. The hospice in this sense flourished along the great pilgrim ways of mediaeval Europe, and the tradition continues in the Holy Cities (Jerusalem, Rome) to this day. The contemporary hospice movement began with Cicely Saunders' vision of integrating this tradition of hospitality with modern scientific medicine in order to create a place of welcome and care for dying people. St Christopher's Hospice in London opened in 1967 as an expression of that vision, and has become an action-parable attracting world-wide attention. The hospice movement has grown rapidly in the United Kingdom, with some eighty programmes currently operating and another thirty in planning stage, while in the USA some twelve hundred programmes are now listed, over 90% of these being established within the last five years. Hospice programmes also operate in Africa, Australia, Canada, India, Sweden and The Netherlands, and no doubt in other countries. Because the hospice movement is loosely linked, one programme being inspired by and building upon another, it is not easy to keep abreast of developments, even in one's own country.

The literature of the hospice movement has been to a large extent couched in anecdotal form,[7] although recently some technical literature has also begun to emerge.[8] There is however substantial agreement in this published material as to the criteria which distinguish hospice care. A fairly comprehensive list is as follows:[9]

ESSENTIALS OF HOSPICE CARE

1. *Management by an experienced clinical team* integrated into the work of the whole medical community and giving effective continuity of care.

2. *Understanding control of the common symptoms of terminal disease, especially pain in all its aspects* will enable patients to live to their maximum potential and will at times herald unexpected remissions and/or the possibility of further active treatment.

3. *Skilled and experienced team nursing* which calls for confident leadership by the ward sister and easy communication among its members.

4. *A full inter-disciplinary staff* meeting frequently for discussion. The doctor does not relinquish his clinical responsibility but a member of another discipline may sometimes assume leadership for a particular patient or family.

5. *A home care programme*, active or consultative and involving all the relevant disciplines, must be developed according to local circumstances so that it can be integrated with the hospitals, the family practices of the area and its own beds.

6. *Recognition of the patient and his family as the unit of care* and of the family as part of the caring team. They may need support, not only in meeting physical demands but also in their own search for reality and meaning.

7. *A mixed group of patients.* Although the current interest in hospice care in the US is especially concerned with 'the dying cancer patient and his family', a good community is usually a mixed one and hospices may include among their concerns those with long-term illness, chronic pain and, in some cases, frailty and old age.

8. *Bereavement follow-up* to identify those who are especially vulnerable and to give support in co-operation with the family doctor and any local services which can be involved.

9. *Methodical recording and analysis* will monitor clinical practice and, co-ordinated with relevant research where possible, lead to soundly based practice and teaching.

10. *Teaching in all aspects of terminal care.* Special units should be a resource, stimulating initial interest, giving experience and passing on tested knowledge to others in both general and specialist fields.

11. *Imaginative use of the architecture available.* Many hospices will not be able to build anew and have to adapt a building in order to combine

privacy with openness and community and a sense of home with efficient operation.

12. *An efficient and approachable administration*, essential to any field of human need and care, is here required to give security to patients, families and staff. Efficiency is both comforting and time saving. So far, hospices have shown that their operation is cost-effective as well as appropriate and humane.

13. *A readiness for the cost of commitment and the search for meaning.* Devotion has been an outstanding characteristic of past and present hospices. Willingness to face this demand has a fundamental bearing on the way the work is done and the stability of the staff. A Christian hospice will be aware of the presence of the crucified and risen Christ in the midst.

A further criterion for most programmes is that patients are admitted on the basis of need, not their ability to pay. Interestingly, one hospice essential which I regard as very important has been omitted from this particular list. This is the use of volunteers in the programme, particularly in supportive services and in visitation and bereavement follow up. While the work of volunteers is essential because of the limited financial resources of many hospices (a majority are charitable organizations), it is also regarded by hospices as a way of increasing public awareness – spreading the gospel of hospice care – and offering support to volunteers, many of whom first come into contact with the hospice as a family member or friend of a dying patient.[10] It should also be noted that since this list was compiled in the late 'seventies home care programmes have increased in significance. It now seems that the dominant form of hospice care is a domiciliary service backed by a limited number of in-patient beds in an associated institution. This of course allows people to do their dying at home, even if the actual last few days of life are spent as an in-patient.

The term hospice thus denotes a model of care, not a set of buildings. As a model of care, hospice care correlates to a significant extent with the characteristics of care that have been emphasized throughout this book. Hospice care is wholistic, employing an interdisciplinary team which includes a patient's family in the caring task as well as offering them support to care and to grieve. Programmes are small enough to be personal, and careful attention is given to communication. There is an understanding of the personal dimension of helping and the cost of that commitment; and there is an awareness of spiritual values and meaning. While not all hospices are religious foundations, they are nevertheless committed to values which are sympathetic to a spiritual outlook on life. A strong case can be made that hospice care is the solution to the concerns and problems I have been examining, at least in so far as finding an appropriate model of terminal care is concerned.

It is not enough simply to suggest that hospice care is the answer to all our problems. Certainly the hospice movement has provided some impressive prototype programmes for terminal care reform. The fact remains, however, that only a tiny proportion of dying people can have access to such programmes at present. If hospice care is as good as it is claimed to be, that fact must be demonstrated, and ways found to link hospice ideals and methods with the dominant structures of care in our health system, the general hospitals and nursing homes.

These are central questions before the hospice movement at the moment: how can effectiveness be measured, preferably in some quantitative sense; and how can hospice care link with existing health care systems? The questions have become urgent with the recent proliferation of hospice programmes in USA, but they are current for every programme in every country. During the 'seventies, while hospice care was establishing its methods, its success seemed self-evident, at least to those sympathetic to its values, and little was done by way of verification and evaluation. This is now an urgent priority as programmes seek wider recognition and funding.

The benefits claimed for hospice care include better pain control, fewer symptoms, improved quality of life and greater satisfaction with care. It is also widely assumed that hospice care with its avoidance of medical heroics will be less costly than other forms of terminal care. To date most evaluations of these benefits have been largely descriptive. The more quantifiable studies which do exist are however not quite so clear cut in their findings. Take for example the comparative study of patients in St Christopher's Hospice with matched patients in neighbouring London hospitals at the end of the 'sixties and again at the end of the 'seventies.[11] In the first of the comparative studies St Christopher's demonstrated significantly better pain relief and overall symptom control than the hospitals, and a better quality of life so far as mobility and mental clarity were concerned. In the second study, however, there was no appreciable difference between hospice and hospital in pain control (hospital performance had improved dramatically) and symptom control was also comparable. Patients and surviving spouses reported less personal distress in both settings in the second study. This improvement in hospital performance is attributed by Parkes to the training in terminal care given by the hospice through its study centre, opened in 1973. Whether or not this is the substantive reason, the study certainly demonstrates a radical improvement in hospital terminal care over the decade. The other significant finding was that spouses were less anxious at the hospice as compared with the hospitals in both parts of the study, and satisfaction with care was greater for hospice than hospitals, although again hospital performance had improved over the intervening decade. The families' preference is attributed by Parkes to the fact that with hospice care the family plays a larger part in care of the patient and is in closer contact with staff both before and after bereavement.

A recent US study attempting to compare hospice with hospital care shows results similar to those of the later Parkes data. Terminal patients at the Veterans Administration Medical Centre, West Los Angeles, were randomized into care in the teaching hospital unit or the hospice unit associated with the hospital.[12] No significant differences were found between the groups in terms of pain control, symptom control, or measures of the quality of life. Hospice patients, however, expressed more satisfaction with the care they received, and patients' families showed somewhat more satisfaction and less anxiety than did the families of those in hospital care.

A comprehensive National Hospice Study is currently in progress in the USA 'to delineate the implications of the inclusion of hospice services in the Medicare program' and to be 'a basis for future Federal fiscal policy and legislation'.[13] To date only preliminary economic evaluations have been published.[14] Reservations have however been expressed about the emphases of the study, particularly its economic focus and its inability to make measurements of the less tangible aspects of patient quality of life, such as a growing spiritual insight.[15] Even the calculation of cost-effectiveness raises some difficult questions: where do you draw the line in estimating costs and savings? For example, one of the clearer findings of the studies already cited is that hospice care provides superior family support. Will this be reflected in better long-term health for these families, bearing in mind the correlation between illness and inadequate or unresolved grief? If in fact families cared for by hospice programmes do have better long-term health prospects, should not this be taken into account in a cost-benefit analysis? And so the discussion continues.

The preliminary economic analysis in the National Hospice Study referred to above indicates that whether hospice care results in reduced costs depends on the type of hospice a patient uses and the length of hospice stay. Home-care-based hospices (those without direct control over inpatient beds) are less costly than hospital-based hospices (those with in-patient beds either in a hospital or a freestanding institution), and both are significantly cheaper than conventional care for an admission of a few weeks. For stays greater than two months, however, hospital-based hospices show cost increases to a level significantly greater than conventional care, while home-care hospice costs remain lower than those of conventional care regardless of the length of stay. Further clarification is awaited, as cost-effectiveness will have profound effects upon how, or if, hospice care will be integrated with existing health care systems.

Findings broadly consistent with these American studies emerge from evaluation of the Citymission Hospice Program in Melbourne, Australia. This hospice programme works in close association with the Oncology Unit of the Royal Melbourne Hospital, a large acute-care teaching hospital, which provides some support services and is the source of the majority of the patients entering the programme. The hospice is however an independent foundation, focussing on domiciliary care with ten palliative care beds in a nursing home operated by the Melbourne Citymission. The programme has recently emerged from a three-year demonstration phase which has been independently evaluated by David Dunt of the Department of Community Medicine, University of Melbourne.[16]

In this study cost-effectiveness has been measured and compared with existing alternative community-based services. A comparison has also been made of the clinical status and satisfaction with care of the patient and the principal caregiver in both types of programme. Over the study period this involved repeated in-depth interviews with sixty-five patients and families from the hospice programme and fifty-five matched patients and families served by other domiciliary nursing services. Findings demonstrate the effectiveness of hospice care, with these patients reporting significantly lower indices of pain, less shortness of breath, and less dissatisfaction with care. The groups did not however differ in emotional symptoms or other quality of life measures. An unexpected finding was that the stress levels of care-givers in the hospice programme were significantly higher than those in alternative domiciliary programmes. A probable explanation for this is that in the demonstration phase particularly consultants have tended to refer to the hospice programme precisely those families who are having the greatest difficulty in coping.

While being shown to be more effective, the care of hospice patients was significantly more expensive than that of patients in existing domiciliary programmes (although of course nowhere near as expensive as in-patient care). The reasons for this were principally the higher nurse to patient ratios of the hospice programme, the fact that hospice patients spent no more time at home and no less time in teaching hospitals than did the control group, and the status of the hospice programme as a new, small demonstration project. With regard to this latter point, indications are that as the programme develops a greater patient load is being handled with only minor increases in staffing costs, so that the direct cost margin between hospice and other domiciliary programmes is decreasing. The evaluation also shows that the cost of admission to the Hospice Palliative Care Unit, by virtue of its location in a nursing home, is significantly less than that of admission to a ward in a teaching hospital. There is then at least the potential for hospice care costs to be more nearly equivalent to those of existing domiciliary programmes which are backed by acute-care hospital services. In general though the evaluation of the Citymission Hospice Program underlines the fact that the case for hospice care cannot be made on purely economic grounds, but must involve judgments concerning the quality of care provided.

The evaluation also raises broader issues in cost-effectiveness which in turn open up questions concerning future directions in terminal care. Dunt points to two assumptions which are often implicit in hospice evaluations: that if a hospice can reduce the amount of hospitalization patients require then this is a saving on the total health bill; and that the establishment costs of services can be neglected in making cost comparisons. Both these assumptions are questionable. What in fact happens when a terminal patient does not occupy a bed in an acute-care hospital is that someone else, perhaps a person on an elective surgery waiting list, does. Thus no immediate saving is involved, but there is actually an increase in overall health expenditure. Nevertheless in this example care is being provided for two people in appropriate contexts – a terminal patient at home and an acute-care patient in an acute-care institution. In the long term a greater commitment to domiciliary services for palliative care should mean less pressure on acute-care beds, a reduction in waiting lists, and thus less need to build new acute-care facilities. It is at this point that hospice care will make its contribution to overall reductions in the health budget, for the establishment costs of acute-care institutions are enormous in comparison with those of hospice or other domiciliary services.

The need for establishment costs to be considered alongside direct care costs also has important implications for the type of palliative care services which are to be offered in the future. That there will need to be an expansion of these services seems clear; in virtually all

Western industrialized nations the average age of the population is increasing, and with this greater proportion of elderly people comes a greater incidence of malignant disease and increased need for palliative care.[17] This will mean both expanding existing programmes and starting new ones. It would appear that the most feasible option economically will be to base new hospice or other palliative care programmes within existing structures. Locating Palliative Care Units in existing hospitals or nursing homes and including hospice services as part of existing domiciliary services will reduce administrative and establishment costs. It is through reasoning like this that a recent review of palliative care services in Victoria has recommended that there be a moratorium on the establishment of free-standing hospices, and that palliative care services which incorporate hospice values and methods be organized on a regional basis from a central acute-care institution.[18] Such a recommendation is not a rejection of hospice care as such, but a recognition of its value together with a desire to see this quality of care available more widely. For in its present form hospice care is accessible only to a few. Even in the United Kingdom with its developed hospice network less than 5% of cancer deaths take place in hospice programmes.[19]

Whither terminal care?

There is consensus among most leaders in hospice care that better terminal care will not be achieved through a proliferation of quasi-independent hospice programmes, but by hospice values and methodology informing and penetrating existing systems of terminal care.[20] There seems also to be an increasing openness among practitioners in conventional care to these hospice-developed values and methods.[21] This is true of the United States as well as the United Kingdom, despite somewhat different paths of development. The hospice movement in Britain has always had largely co-operative relationships with practitioners in other areas of care. In the USA by way of contrast many hospice programmes have consciously maintained a distinction between themselves and conventional structures. Hospice care has tended to be associated with an anti-institutional, anti-technological stream of thought, so that for example physician leadership of a hospice team is uncommon.[22] Even so, hospice ideals are increasingly being taken into conventional care, and many hospitals are including a hospice-style team as a part of their services.

As we have already noted, the practical impact of this merging of hospice with conventional forms of care has resulted in overall improvements in the quality of terminal care in Western society.

Hospice programmes have served as models of excellence, have provided venues for training practitioners of a variety of disciplines in terminal care, and have raised public awareness of the creative possibilities inherent even in the final stage of life. In many ways the hospice movement has been a recall to common-sense fundamentals of care. Through it we have learned a great deal about death itself, and what it is like to die or have someone you love die with cancer. We have learned a great deal about how to care for dying people and their families. In so doing we have learned a great deal about ourselves; and we have begun to learn more about life. These 'learned truths',[23] have resulted in a simple yet effective programme for care of the dying. This programme has been developed in the pioneering hospices such as St Christopher's and St Joseph's, and is now replicated in programmes all around the world. The process of learning about death and dying has also contributed to a renewed interest in the art of caring. The general social awareness of and interest in the 'new' terminal care has been one of the important contemporary influences shifting the focus from technical expertise to the quality of personal care offered in professional relationships. This shift in focus and values is quietly and effectively improving the quality of care throughout the health services, not merely in the area of terminal care alone.

Thus the transfer of values and techniques from hospice care into other forms of terminal care and indeed care in general is already proceeding informally. The questions for the coming years are how this transfer can be undertaken systematically in designing new palliative care services, and what this might mean for hospice programmes, both those already operating and those currently in the planning stage.

One approach to these questions has already been alluded to; that of the review of palliative care services in Victoria. The review committee recommends that regionalized palliative care services be established, based on every major general hospital throughout the state and geared to domiciliary care with the object of allowing the patient to remain at home as long as it is appropriate. The committee also recommends that palliative care services from each hospital should be co-ordinated by a senior medical officer, usually a physician with experience in oncology; that the home-care service should include twenty-four-hour medical and nursing cover (not just nursing cover alone); that the service provide out-patient consulting facilities and be backed with in-patient beds in the hospital or a hospice; and that bereavement follow-up be an integral part of the task. Terminal care is thus seen as a responsibility of the general hospital, which provides co-ordination and support services. It is further recommended that there be no further establishment of hospice-type institutions, but that the principles of hospice care be applied in the development of palliative care based on existing hospitals. The committee also notes the need for greater education in the area of death and dying in all health professional courses, and postgraduate training for those wishing to be associated with a palliative care programme.

When reading through their detailed report it can readily be seen that the insights and recommendations of the committee are grounded in the experience and discoveries of the hospice movement; and they are quick to acknowledge this fact. The proposed moratorium on hospice development thus has more to do with a desire to integrate terminal care with existing services than to diminish the contribution a hospice might make. The committee sees existing hospices as continuing to operate within the broader regional palliative care framework, making a special contribution in the areas of research and education.

In broad outline such a proposal appears to have merit, especially in its intention to make expert terminal care available to all. However, there will no doubt be many practical difficulties as the recommendations are implemented over the next decade. For example, it remains to be seen if a regional approach to palliative care will be able to retain the small, stable, personal teams which are essential to hospice practice, or whether these will degenerate into loosely-linked networks which are unable to support hospice values and methods. This will inevitably happen if regions are too large or case loads too heavy; for hospice practice requires that the participants in a programme – team, patients and families – know each other and relate primarily as people, not through practitioner and patient roles. Too large a programme makes this personal dimension practically impossible. There are significant difficulties too in locating Palliative Care Units (PCUs) within existing acute-care institutions. To do so will remove a significant number of beds from acute-care use, and add to the pressures already on the hospitals. Hospital administration will be tempted to move other non-terminal patients in and out of the PCU as beds are available, use PCU staff to relieve in other areas of the hospital, or staff the PCU from the general pool rather than maintain an identifiable team which will care for patients both when they are in the PCU and when they are at home. Any or all of these would have a deleterious effect on the quality of terminal care provided. Of course these objections are not insuperable obstacles; but they do imply that the principal medical officer co-ordinating palliative care in each region will have to be an exceptional person to make the scheme work in the face of the many competing pressures upon it. I am not convinced that we have sufficient physicians possessing the necessary experience and vision to ensure that the recommendations are actually realized.

While these recommendations were generated in an Australian context, with little or no reference so far as I am aware to palliative care planning in other countries, it is interesting to see that they follow directions similar to those already emerging in the United Kingdom and the United States. It is clear that hospice care is no longer to be regarded as an alternative to other forms of terminal care, an option available to a few dying people who, through accident of geography or special need, are able to gain access to it. Rather, in the interests of better terminal care the hospices must re-integrate with the system from which they initially withdrew to pursue their vision. Only in this way will it become possible to offer better terminal care to all dying people and their families. It is not possible for hospices as largely-charitable institutions to service a whole population; this can only be done through proper co-operation within the total health care system.

However, it is essential that hospices continue to function in very much their present form. It would be a tragedy indeed if wider co-operation in a palliative care network forced hospices to take on much larger case loads with minimal increases in staff numbers, or lose contact with their community so that the involvement and interest of volunteers was affected. In any wider programme of palliative care the hospices are needed as models of excellence, achieving standards in care with which other programmes can compare themselves. To this end hospices will need to develop and refine their documentation and research activities, so that evaluations and comparisons can be clearly made. The teaching role of hospices will also become increasingly important, both their training role with professionals working in palliative care, and their training of volunteers to work in terminal care within the hospice or with other palliative care units in the community.

Perhaps the principal difficulties in regionalizing palliative care services will arise from decisions about scale. I believe that it is crucial for palliative care teams to remain small, cohesive groups, dealing with a fairly small patient load (of the order of thirty to fifty patient and family units), preferably within a defined local area. Such numbers are large enough to be viable economically, but small enough for participants in the programme to maintain a sense of personal identity and belonging. This is an essential aspect of hospice care, and hospices will need to resist any pressures to expand their operations past the point where a sense of community occurs naturally within the programme. Whilst certain hospice methodologies can be isolated and described, I do not believe that they can be transferred effectively from the community context of the hospice into another context in which community does not exist. It is the quality of relationships which is central to hospice care; without community hospice techniques can have little effect.

I think that, just as studying the end of life teaches us a great deal about life itself, so looking at terminal care teaches us more about what it means to care in general. In the final analysis better terminal care relies upon the ability of professional staff to really care, something which is only possible within continuing relationships and with the support of a committed team. Present health care structures do not make this quality of care easy to achieve, for professional training and practice tends to focus upon technical expertise more than upon capacity for relationship and upon autonomy more than upon interdependence. The quest for better terminal care – in fact better care in general – requires us to look seriously at revising our present understandings of professional identity and practice.

7

· *Professional Care and Pastoral Care* ·

Throughout this book I have talked about helping relationships without distinguishing clearly between those relationships a person has with professional helpers and the relationships in which he is helped by his family and friends. In that this discussion has focussed around issues of control and the way these affect the relationship it has not been necessary to do so; both professional helpers and the family and friends of a person needing help are people with power who can exert control on the relationship. However, the source and nature of that power is different. Family or friends have power through their established relationship with the person in crisis. It is power based on personal knowledge and shared experience, which can be used creatively to deepen the relationship and bring insight to present experience, or coercively to avoid its pain. Few people will continue to raise unwelcome issues in the face of concerted opposition from family and friends, for in doing so they risk alienating the people with whom their identity is invested, the people who offer the only apparent support in the present crisis. Professional power in contrast has a different origin. It is not based on personal knowledge and shared history but upon accredited training and socially-accepted criteria which are seen to be objective in contrast with the subjective power exerted by family and friends. This professional power too can be used creatively or coercively, reinforcing or opposing the power exerted by family and friends. My argument of course is that power needs to be acknowledged and used to liberate rather than coerce, to explore options rather than control and reinforce the person's helplessness.

The family and friendship power structure for most dying people is well-established and probably not amenable to much modification, for the participants are seldom self-conscious or particularly reflective about the way they interact. The professional power structure, however, should be more open to influence, being formed through training and open to evaluation as part of established professional practice. Through changes to the nature and quality of professional relationships it may be possible to deal with some of the destructive and coercive aspects of professional helping relationships, and trust that the resultant changes in professional practice and institutional structures will in turn influence general social expectations concerning the giving and receiving of help.

To this point I have been writing as if the character of a professional relationship can be described clearly in terms of the professional person's identity and powers. In fact this is not the case; even the term 'professional' is subject to a wide variety of understandings and interpretations,[1] and the powers available vary considerably from profession to profession. Many of the current attempts at defining what constitutes a profession rely on specifying traits which set professions apart from other occupations. For example: a professional is 1. a broadly educated person, 2. possessing highly developed skills and knowledge, 3. working under the discipline of an ethic developed and enforced by a body of peers, and 4. commissioned to satisfy complex needs by making judgments entailing dangerous consequences.[2] Definitions like this focus on training, ethical standards and self-regulation as characterizing a professional approach. They do not, however, offer insight into the social dynamics of professionalism – the process whereby an occupation becomes a profession or for that matter lapses from professional status – nor do they help in understanding the growing professionalization of our society, particularly in the health and welfare area. As we have seen, this latter feature creates significant problems in terminal care. I would go further and suggest that it diminishes the quality of professional care in general. As professionalism and specialization increase people under care find themselves removed further from the everyday support of their community, their needs being addressed by a number of professionals of different disciplines who maintain only cursory communication with one another.

An alternative understanding of professionalism in terms of its social function is given by Wilding in his analysis of professional power.[3] His approach is one of suspicion, seeing professionalism essentially as the pursuit and maintenance of social privilege and power. Thus the construction of a professional ethic, seen as a public safeguard by most of the trait definitions, is regarded by Wilding more as a campaign document in the pursuit of professional self-interest. The process of professionalization thus begins in occupational self-assertion, leading on to struggle, conflict and, if successful, to a position of social domination in which the group achieves monopoly in its occupational area and virtual autonomy in regulating it. These privileges of monopoly and self-regulation are regarded by the profession as necessary conditions for the proper fulfilment of their work. Clearly they are in the interests of the professionals; whether they are always in the best interests of society is less than clear.

In Wilding's understanding professional status is expressed in specific powers: the power to make and administer policy; to define a client's needs and problems; to allocate resources; to control the area of work; and consequently to assume power over people.[4] Such powers are most clearly evidenced and documented for the medical profession, but as Wilding shows they can be demonstrated in the approach of almost all other professions in our welfare-oriented Western society.

Thus in our society health and welfare policy is shaped almost exclusively by professional associations. Consumer groups are frequently ignored altogether, and even when they are consulted their opinions are seldom given much weight. The effect of pressure from the medical profession upon the National Health Service in Britain or the Medicare schemes in Australia bear ample witness to this, and also illustrate the ways in which the interests of a dominant profession can override those of other professions, such as nursing or social work, which cannot aspire to the same degree of autonomy or power. A further crucial aspect of professional practice is the assumption of the power to give a client what he really needs rather than what he wants. Thus a professional will assume the right to redefine a person's presenting problem and offer treatment appropriate to this redefinition. Of course this may well be valid and helpful; but the narrowness of professional vision can equally work against the client's interests. The professional's commitment in most instances to an individual therapeutic relationship can ignore important social or political dimensions to a problem. And of course the tendency is always to re-define a problem to bring it within the area of the professional's expertise rather than pursue it on a co-operative interdisciplinary basis.

This narrowness of vision continues as an issue in the allocation of resources and professional self-regulation in general. A considerable proportion of health and welfare funds are allocated by decisions made in individual consultation with clients. Thus expenditure is determined by totalling these individual decisions, which often are not related to each other in any systematic way or balanced against alternative possibilities for promoting health and welfare not presented through client consultations. Further, expenditure is directed primarily to those who are able and know how to ask for professional help, and is highest in the areas with the highest concentrations of professionals. These areas are both geographical – as witness the difficulty involved in filling professional posts in remote or economically-depressed regions – and areas of specialization. Certain 'popular' sub-disciplines attract a preponderance of professional interest and funding: in medicine these are hospital-centred technical disciplines like surgery and intensive care medicine rather than community-oriented disciplines like geriatrics or terminal care; in social work family therapy is far more appealing than probation work, and so on. These images of popularity are not adequately related to the actual need in the community, but the pattern persists because of the tradition of self-regulation among the professions. Professions control the selection, training and admission of candidates to their ranks; the process of training tends to reinforce established professional attitudes and interests; and professionals are responsible for their own ongoing assessment. Social accountability is diluted by these privileges, and any political attempts to arrange a more equitable distribution of resources and personnel are met with strong resistance, including in recent times industrial action, from professional groups.

Professionals in particular will want to protest that this analysis is biased and overlooks a great deal of the positive contribution which professionals make through responsible, ethical care of individuals in society. I would not disagree with this protest, but would argue that the analysis still highlights critical problems with professionalism which cannot lightly be dismissed.

In resisting social accountability professionals seem to be clinging to an idealized self-image. Increasingly we hear from professional organizations that professional practice is a vocation in which money-earning capacity is secondary to service; that in any case the financial remuneration received is commensurate with the long and arduous training undergone in pursuit of professional qualification; that peer evaluation is a completely adequate safeguard of client interests and therefore that any attempted political intervention must be motivated by prejudice or bad faith; that the status and power of professions within society is an appropriate recognition of their ethical integrity and record of disinterested service of society. I suggest that these are idealized statements; not that they are wrong, but that they are only part of the truth. There is also evidence that a number of professionals command a disproportionately high income, much of it derived from public monies; that the length and content of training has as much to do with professional status requirements as with actual effectiveness;

that peer evaluation is lax and frequently almost non-existent, so that only the grossest of abuses are challenged; and that ethical service is not always the primary consideration in actual professional practice.[5] The dilemma I see is that this conscious idealism actually contributes to abuses of power. A far more realistic self-understanding is vital for any sort of resolution of the conflict between service and self-interest. I will discuss this dilemma in self-understanding a little later. First I want to focus upon another problem of our current professional structures; their failure to take proper account of the corporate dimension of professional responsibility.

Fundamentally, I believe that our professional structures are no longer adequate for today's society. The professional model we have is derived from a bygone era of private practice in which independent professionals contracted with independent clients to deliver services provided wholly by the professional and paid for by the client. Professional association then was largely a matter of mutual recognition and fellowship; welfare relied upon an individual professional's benevolence in moderating or waiving a fee or co-operating with the many voluntary welfare organizations which abounded. In this situation an individual ethic was well able to express responsible professional behaviour. Today, however, the situation is vastly different. In the health and welfare field, instead of the single profession of medicine, we have a number of associated disciplines which model their practice on that of medicine and not infrequently come into conflict with one another in demarcation disputes. Such disputes usually arise in formulating policy and setting up procedures, and are frequently solved at that level; although it seems that increasingly they are giving rise to industrial action by professionals. One effect of this is to transform professional associations into political lobby groups committed to their own particular interests. No longer can an individual practitioner offer services of which he is the direct and sole provider; public funds are extensively involved in professional training and in everyday professional practice. Even the operation of so-called 'private' medicine relies heavily upon public-funded health care facilities and programmes. Welfare is largely a Government responsibility with voluntary organizations playing a greatly-reduced role.

These changes and the rapid growth of technical expertise in the various disciplines have also had a profound effect on the professional helping relationship. No longer can a client expect to deal with only one or two professionals, except for the simplest of procedures. Increasing specialization means that a number of professionals are involved at different stages of a serious or critical situation. Because of this, and because of the focus upon institutional care with its interchangeability of personnel, there is less opportunity for a client to build a relationship with a trusted practitioner. Even where there is a continuing primary relationship, with a general practitioner for example, the effectiveness of this relationship is undercut by the difficulties involved in assessing the differing perspectives of different specialists and the relatively poor communication which exists between professionals. This whole situation is further compounded by the increasingly medical orientation of our society, meaning that a huge variety of human problems turn up in doctors' consulting rooms when in fact they require alternative approaches; a good neighbour, a more satisfying job, a spiritual director. . . Of course the diagnosis of such needs is not always easy, and referral is extremely difficult. Thus while medical practitioners are aware of the problem it is still easier to adopt a medical approach than to tell people to look elsewhere. But this reinforces the dominance of a medical perspective and enhances the power base of the professionals.

To move beyond this situation towards a more appropriate professionalism will not be easy. It will involve changing the perceptions of professionals and of society in general; in particular achieving a more realistic perception of what the different professions can and cannot do. It will mean professionals recognizing their responsibility to society and setting up procedures to make themselves more directly accountable in terms of public expenditure, responsible interaction with other professions, and the mode of service offered to society. It will involve a re-examination of the professional's relationship with clients. It will include a better assessment of the aims of professional practice. If the professions are to be enabling rather than disabling disciplines, then there needs to be a clearer focus upon empowering the client; for with the present ethic it appears that professionals can function quite legitimately while keeping clients dependent on their services.

Thus professional ethics need to incorporate a goal of justice at the corporate level and of liberation of the individual at the personal level.[6] Such a stance differs from the present one of professional beneficence – doing good for the client. To look for justice involves some sort of assessment of the client's interests in the light of wider social needs. To look for liberation involves some vision of a client's human potential and understanding of whether his requirements will help him realize that potential or block him from moving towards it. Horrobin points out in his critique of Illich that a professional stance like this requires professionals to be more aware that the cumulative effect of their decisions has a deep impact upon society, and that this consciousness must be brought into medical decision-making.[7] I think Horrobin is right; but I do not agree where he appears to suggest that reform within the professions will be adequate to bring this about. Social accountability must be introduced and power must be shared, so that valid professional insight and expertise is balanced with social vision. For this to happen, professionalism must be understood in terms of partnership with clients and with society in general.

This concept of partnership must recognize the mutual contributions of the professions and society; of the different professions to one another; and of professionals with their clients. In the health and welfare area particularly this aspect is crucial. While professionals working in this area can 'deliver' care, they cannot 'deliver' health or welfare to their clients. Where this comes about it emerges as a result of co-operative action – partnership – between professional and client. As this comment implies, such partnership must go a long way further than the sharing of information, important though that is. It must be expressed in the sharing of power so that those who use professional services have a genuine input into the structure and practice of those services, learning in their relationships with professional helpers to care for themselves and take responsibility for their own lives.

I do not however wish to be seen as espousing Illich's utopian vision of a de-professionalized society in which mutual self-care by the laity is encouraged and recognized legally as a preferred alternative to professional expertise.[8] Professional expertise is needed. The issue is one of changing both professional and popular consciousness, and expressing these changes in revised structures. These should balance a narrow professional focus with a broad social vision, client responsibility with professional autonomy, and transform the competing interests of different professions into a co-operative stance. Wilding summarizes it thus:

> The partnership with society which could lead to the total subordination of a profession to public purposes is balanced by the profession's partnership with individuals, so that the profession does not become the slave of government. Similarly, stress on the partnership of a profession with other professions can be a check on the professional partnership with individual clients.
>
> The professions are both the servants of society and the servants of individuals. They can only succeed in their work if the dual nature of the responsibility is welcomed and if the basis of the relationship is accepted as one of partnership.[9]

Wilding, however, seems content to accept *an* explanation of professional practice in terms of self-interest as an adequate explanation of professional motivation in general. While accepting much of his analysis I am unwilling to set aside other more altruistic motives which direct and inform professional action. So it is interesting to find another study which explores the partnership theme from a more positive appreciation of professional practice. Alastair Campbell suggests that what professional carers have to offer society in return for the obvious advantages which they receive from it is 'moderated love'.[10] By this he means a skilful balance between attachment and detachment in the helping relationship and a symbolic mediation of concern and hope even in the midst of dire illness and distress.[11] This is demonstrated as brotherliness in medicine, companionship in nursing, and hopefulness in social work. These qualities he sees as characteristics of love, transcending personal advantage or professional advancement.

Medical brotherliness is a love which fosters friendship, neither objectifying a patient as an 'interesting case' nor seeking the god-like domination which makes medicine a form of idolatry. Rather, brotherliness causes professional power to share control, encouraging the patient to take part in the shared task of understanding and dealing with the illness as it affects his personal being. Similarly nursing offers companionship, a relationship which exists while a joint purpose is pursued, characterized by sharing but not imposition, allowing the companion to make his or her own journey. This calls for costly commitment – being with not just doing to the patient – although it is a commitment limited to the declared purpose of the relationship, be it restoration to strength and independence or a journey into death. It is a love which requires balance, for either an absence or an excess of detachment may destroy it. Hopefulness is the aspect of love offered in social work relationships, where that relationship itself is the primary medium of care. The hope demonstrated is that through the relationship this person may discover a renewed sense of self-worth, freedom, purpose, a way to transform problems into possibilities. This hopefulness is prepared to confront the political issues raised by individuals' dilemmas, but still sees the need for personal change to be pursued as the foundation for structural or political goals.

Again, as Campbell points out, the affirmation of such qualities in professional practice requires a change in professional self-understanding and in popular thought; for changes will be met with resistance from the people who want to maintain their illusions about themselves or about life, both within and without the professions.

There are those who do not want to be reminded that they are mortal and vulnerable; who want to believe that there are simple and practical solutions to all of life's problems; who want to avoid taking responsibility for their own destiny and the struggle this often entails.

The actual structures which might result from a partnership approach to professional practice would vary according to each situation and the professions represented. It would require a careful analysis of the levels of decision-making involved, and the establishment of appropriate means of accountability for each level. For example, the overall allocation of health and welfare resources is fundamentally a government responsibility on which professional and community groups might offer advice but which they cannot expect to control directly. When it comes to the deployment of resources at a local community level it would be appropriate to involve a variety of concerned members of that community, professional and lay, in the decision-making. At another level much decision-making will be done by professionals in consultation, for there is obviously little appropriate lay input to an immediate decision as to the best surgical procedure to follow or the best drug regime to employ. Nevertheless it would be appropriate to have some form of lay participation in the ongoing evaluation and assessment of routine professional practice: an articulate lay perspective can usefully challenge unexamined professional assumptions and open up fresh approaches, even in relatively technical areas, for scientific method is not the peculiar possession of health and welfare professionals. Hospital ethics committees offer one model for such lay moderation in the area of research activities. Team functioning as discussed in the previous chapter is another practical example of partnership.

I have already suggested, however, that a fundamental barrier to partnership is the attitude of professionals in separating themselves from lay and client groups, an attitude which treats these other people as somehow different. This attitude stems I believe from self-idealization, the tendency professional people have not only to promote a public image of personal dedication and selfless service, but also to believe their own propaganda. Adopting such an idealized image at a conscious level causes us to suppress other aspects of our personal motivations – our desires for control of our relationships, for power and status – so that these operate at a largely unconscious level of our personality. This in turn sets up a stressful cycle in which we strive to make our everyday behaviour consistent with our idealized self-image, displacing or suppressing non-ideal responses to our clients such as our anger or impatience with them, our sexual attraction to or repulsion from them.

Inevitably then we are not truly engaged as persons in the relationship, and we may become aware of the gap between our professed ideals and our actual attitudes and practice. Consciousness of that gap increases our sense of inadequacy and guilt, and usually leads us to drive ourselves harder in the pursuit of 'ideal' performance. This simply does not work. Either we continue to struggle; or we cope by distancing ourselves from our own inner world; or we rebel. Struggle is usually shown in recurring stress symptoms and eventual 'burn out'. Distancing ourselves from our inner world leads to the non-reflective practice of our profession and perhaps to some crisis in which the repressed emotional contents of our minds exact their dues. Rebellion usually takes the form of an abuse of professional trust: doctors become addicted to narcotic drugs or fraudulently manipulate their income; lawyers abscond with the trust funds; clergymen become sexually involved with parishioners. . . None of these is a particularly creative response to the stress of professional practice! Rather, we need to tackle the problem at its source; the idealized self-image which we adopt and promote, sometimes actively, sometimes passively by accepting without question the idealized projections of our clients.

This dilemma is focussed by the Jungian analyst Adolf Guggenbühl-Craig in his discussion of power in the helping professions.[12] He contends that the more an idealized model is held to at the conscious level the more firmly its opposite is constellated in the unconscious. The effect then is that the unconscious shadow intrudes upon the helping relationship to distort and undermine the conscious striving for excellence. The greater the idealization and striving the greater the distortion. Professional shadow selves are seen in the social caricatures of various professional roles; the doctor as charlatan, the clergyman as hypocrite, the teacher as unworldly and childish. These shadow selves are not adopted deliberately; rather the doctor becomes a charlatan because he wants to heal as many people as possible while the clergyman becomes a hypocrite and false prophet because he wants to bring as many people as possible to the true faith. This desire drives them to overpower their patients or parishioners, coercion which is all the more seductive because of the obvious sincerity of purpose behind it. Yet the sincerity of such a doctor or minister is misleading; he is in fact working for himself, not his client.

This dilemma cannot be resolved by conscious effort or learned strategies alone. These reinforce and entrench the abuse of professional power. Resolution lies outside the sphere of specifically professional activity; only a professional who is passionately involved in his own life can help clients to find theirs. A professional can only avoid seeking to meet his own basic needs in his relationships with clients if those needs are being met with his family and friends.

To seek to meet needs in client relationships introduces distortion because these relationships are inevitably asymmetric. In an area that matters the professional has power which is not available to the client, and while mutuality is the goal of the relationship it cannot be truly mutual from the beginning while it is focussed around the task of meeting the client's need. Mutuality can develop if the professional is willing to limit himself, make room for the client to grow and assume power in his own life. If the professional has a deep need to assume and retain some power over the other, the relationship cannot help the client (or the professional for that matter) to grow emotionally and spiritually to more than a limited extent. In some sorts of client-professional relationships of course this probably doesn't matter (except that the professional never becomes the person he might be). If for example I have a broken leg I am probably not going to require from my doctor anything more than expert physical attention. But if I need extended care, as in terminal illness, I may have emotional and spiritual needs to be met by the people who care for me on a professional basis. If there is distortion through those carers' needs, my needs will not be met in a way which will support me to grow and find meaning in my dying.

Guggenbühl-Craig suggests that distortions in helping relationships arise because of a distortion of the unconscous motivation which initially attracts health care professionals to their vocation.[13] Within each person there is both a healer and a patient – we have powerful resources for care and deep needs to be met. Problems arise when for example a doctor can see himself only as a healer, and not recognize the patient within, his own woundedness and need. This doctor will endeavour to dominate his patients in an attempt to meet externally a need which is actually internal, the need to restore relationship between the healer and patient within. This need will in fact be met not through exercising power over patients but when the doctor pays attention to his own repressed pain. These problems are compounded when such a doctor meets a patient who has lost contact with the healer within and is prepared to be totally passive and compliant, waiting to be healed without accepting any responsibility for healing himself. Such a patient will welcome domination for it seems to hold out an external solution to an inner dilemma, his lost capacity to will his own health.

Professional relationships alone are not enough to keep a professional in contact with the patient within, for as we have already noted these relationships are asymmetric. In them the healing role of the professional is emphasized, and the other takes the patient role. It becomes easy for the professional to ignore or explain away any patient who is not compliant, who challenges authority or makes the professional uneasy. Professional understanding enables us to rationalize away criticism or confrontation which might otherwise awaken us to our inner inadequacy and pain. For balance to be maintained, for a professional to be a 'wounded healer' who strives to constellate the healing factor within his patients while remaining in touch with his own woundedness, that professional must continually be challenged by something which can neither be mastered nor fended off by his professional attitudes and techniques. The only way for this to happen is for the professional to be committed as a person to a community, usually the community of family and friends, in which his relationships are symmetrical so that he is challenged as well as consulted, reproached for his failings as well as praised for his virtues, affirmed for himself and not merely for his professional actions. Only through this continuing interchange with people with whom he shares relationships based on love can a professional continue to encounter his shadow side and maintain the balance which will permit emotional and spiritual growth for both himself and his patients.

These reflections on professionalism have profound implications for professional training. The critique I have offered highlights significant problems in the areas of social responsibility and personal formation – areas which are addressed only obliquely in formal training courses. I would argue that personal formation should be central to professional training; and in that such formation properly includes a corporate dimension it should take account of social responsibility too. I believe that in the helping professions a person's motives and self-understanding matter as much as technical skill in caring. Formation should not be left to chance, but should be addressed in the selection, training and professional accreditation of candidates as well as through regular professional review.

Attention to personal qualities needs to begin in the selection of candidates for training. Currently most professions select candidates on the sole basis of academic achievement, which may have little to do with any vocational sense or suitability for the actual practice of the profession. A consequence in the case of medicine is, Horrobin suggests, that we are 'breeding a profession whose major concerns are academic empire building on the one hand, and the rapid accumulation of wealth on the other'.[14] While this may be thought a somewhat extreme claim, it is at least clear that in the present system there are virtually no safeguards to prevent it from happening. Since failure rates in most professional training courses are low, selection for training is strongly linked with eventual accreditation. On this basis alone selection should be taken more seriously than it is, with some strenuous attempt being made to establish, through interview and references, a candidate's vocational sense and personal suitability for training and eventual professional practice. Introducing a different set of values and criteria for selection like this would no doubt still exclude some good candidates who happened not to present themselves appropriately; but so does the present system exclude many people who one cannot help feeling would make better practitioners than some of those who actually gain selection in courses. Perhaps one way towards compensating for initial selection errors would be to offer a 'second chance' by guaranteeing a certain number of places in training courses for students around thirty years of age. The introduction of students with greater experience and maturity could scarcely fail to be of benefit to the training groups and to the profession in general. Of course in some helping professions already a significant number of candidates are people in the middle years of life, and this recent trend shows little sign of abating.

A further aid to improved training would be a careful assessment of what content and level of training is actually needed for competent professional practice. Again to take medicine as an example, it would seem that a significant proportion of doctors' time is spent on tasks for which they have little or no formal training (terminal care being one example!) or for which they are significantly over-trained (to what extent does a GP utilize his training in hospital technology?) A similar situation obtains for other professions (such as nursing) as they seek to increase their status through extending courses of training and relocating those courses in Universities or Tertiary Colleges. One effect of all this seems to be that ordinary caring tasks are devalued or neglected. The mode of selection and type of training is producing students who are motivated towards specialization, research, and achievement of professional status more than people who will seek to meet the actual needs confronting their profession in today's society.

To give attention to personal formation alongside the acquiring of knowledge and developing of professional skills would require a change of emphasis in professional education in general. It would mean moving away from an instructional model of delivering knowledge (teaching) towards one in which students taking a greater responsibility for their learning and professional development. An important component of this would be supervised reflection upon experience, structured situations in which students reflect both with an individual supervisor and in supervised groups upon the personal impact of their learning, their feelings about what they have discovered and experienced and the impact of this new learning upon their self-understanding and world-view. Hopefully in this way self-understanding might be developed in conjunction with and through professional growth; and even more importantly students would learn disciplines of self-supervision so that personal reflection upon experience would continue as an integral part of professional practice.

It would be important also that a significant part of training be in interdisciplinary groups. If team work is to have an adequate basis of mutual professional understanding this should begin to be formed in student days. Interdisciplinary supervised groups and interdisciplinary case-work learning should contribute significantly to developing a generation of professionals who can appreciate each others' disciplinary perspective and contribution.

The process of supervision and review should not stop at the point of professional qualification. There needs to be some sort of ongoing accountability and review. In a certain sense this occurs in the market place; incompetent or overbearing practitioners soon become known and discriminating people avoid them. However, the professions themselves continue to tolerate a fair number of poorly skilled, largely incompetent, out-of-touch practitioners within their ranks. While those who blatantly infringe in matters of individual ethics find themselves confronted by their peers, the sub-standard practitioner tends to be left alone. A process of professional review, say at five-year intervals, could be helpful in maintaining standards of professional competence and vocational commitment. Such a process might not be universally welcomed by professionals, but it could be an important move in regaining some measure of community confidence in the commitment of professionals to their ideals of service at a time when there is a growing tide of cynicism concerning professional self-interest and the level of professional earnings.

A further aspect which needs careful reassessment is the degree to which professional training is based in and around large institutions. There are certain advantages in this, of course – the variety of experience offered to the students is an obvious one. But it also means that we are in effect turning out professionals whose expectation and ideals are shaped by the large institution, when we need professionals who are competent and willing to work within small, community-based, community-accountable structures. Only through structures like this will we be able to regain a truly personal dimension to health care and find a meaningful social and professional accountability. I will return to this point in the closing section, meanwhile noting here that the hospice is one example of an institution which relies upon limited size to make possible the growth of real relationships and a sense of solidarity among patients, family and staff. Supportive care and elements of community accountability appear naturally within such a programme.

Professionalism and pastoral care

Although I have made use of the views of a variety of commentators in discussing professionalism, my critique is based once again on a pastoral perspective. Among my fundamental assumptions are that the quality of care offered in a helping relationship depends upon a helper's commitment to continuing personal development as well as upon helping skills he may have acquired; that a helper will work to further a client's capacity to take responsibility for his or her own life and relationships; and that proper care will aim at building a community in which people can find a place to belong and an opportunity to give as well as to receive. Such assumptions are of course derived from the pastoral criteria set out in chapter 3.

Clearly a professional person's power within a helping relationship may be used to achieve such pastoral goals. But it may equally well be used to oppose them through exerting control on the relationship. That is, professionalism as such is not to be uncritically endorsed from a pastoral point of view. In fact pastoral objectives will be frustrated if professional identity is used – as it frequently is – in a competitive or containing way, or if professional status is used to set oneself over against other groups of people, seeking to control them or to establish privilege more than accept responsibility. A narrow or exclusive professional focus may fail to recognize the extent or variety of another person's need, issuing in inadequate, irrelevant or even harmful treatment and 'care'. Professionalism may emphasize technical skill at the expense of personal formation and responsibility. It may focus on the delivery of services rather than the service of people. It may be expressed in institutional forms which benefit principally the professionals – that is, we may find ourselves identified with the oppressors rather than the oppressed. In all these ways professionalism can undermine and oppose pastoral goals.

Equally, however, professionalism may be used in the pursuit of pastoral objectives. When abuses of power like those listed above are avoided, professional power may be used to encourage interdependence and team functioning – that is, to build a sense of community which expresses itself in co-operative action. Then professional power may be used to share knowledge and facilitate health rather than to protect professional insights for reasons of personal advantage. Professional power can open up the wider dimensions of a person's need and potential, initiating or re-awakening growth and helping that person discover a vocation and purpose in life.

It seems appropriate at this stage to point to the ambiguous possibilities of professionalism in pastoral care as there have been strands within the modern pastoral movement which emphasize the need for professional development while remaining rather uncritical of the professional models they are adopting. Thus for example pastoral counselling has tended to draw heavily upon the language and methodology of psychotherapy (particularly in the USA) or social casework (particularly in the UK) with little critical attention being given to the wider implications of such borrowing. All too often it has led to a form of professional specialization which has separated counselling from other aspects of Christian ministry, and distanced pastoral counsellors from both the support of and accountability to a local faith community. In turn this separation has distorted the ability of such counselling to be truly pastoral. In institutional settings the focus on developing professional skills in pastoral care has tended to identify pastors with the staff rather than with the clients, reducing or nullifying the pastor's mediating role, his or her focus upon the shared humanity which lies behind the other distinctions highlighted in the institutional context.

None of these comments is intended to call into question the acquisition of specific skills to be used in pastoral work. I affirm the need for the pastoral disciplines to make use of the best possible resources for care, including insights and skills developed in other helping disciplines. The issue I am addressing here rather is the danger of also adopting certain professional attitudes and methods which are inimical to a pastoral perspective. This can happen in quite subtle ways. Not many pastors would uncritically adopt the management techniques of some health professions, rightly seeing these as imposing controls which are inappropriate if relationships are to be truly pastoral. Yet borrowing the terminology of these professions for use in pastoral work can have something of the same effect, for much professional language tends to objectify 'clients' or 'patients', distancing the helper from the one seeking help, emphasizing the helper's control of the situation through terminology access-ible to him but not to the person coming for help.

It is probably not necessary to develop this aspect of the discussion further. A number of useful critiques making the same point are available elsewhere.[15] It is, however, encouraging to note a significant trend in the pastoral literature of the last few years towards a rediscovery of our pastoral heritage and ways in which this may be integrated with the skills and insights of the modern helping professions. Thus the resources of scripture, spiritual formation and Christian community increasingly are being re-introduced to pastoral practice as an organizing framework, in contrast to earlier approaches where the framework tended to be that of psychotherapy or social casework into which some religious terminology and insight was inserted.

The pastoral focus upon care as building community becomes for the professional pastor the tasks of fostering community within the church and with professionals in other helping disciplines, as well as with peers. The latter task is readily acknowledged as a part of professional practice; the former tasks are not, and as we have already seen much professional practice is directed towards maintaining distinctions in these areas rather than in building community. Within the church then pastoral professionals need to be aware of the continuity between the care they offer and the care offered by the whole congregation. While professional pastoral care may utilize particular skills not available to other members of the faith community – or not developed in the same way – it does not offer a different kind of care. Professional pastoral skills and the resources of the caring congregation complement each other. All aspects of care, professional and lay, co-operate to equip and serve the faith community. Professional training should not divide or create a hierarchy within the church's caring ministries. Professionals too need to recognize the source of their care within the faith community, and seek nourishment there in mutually responsible relationships within the congregation. A willingness to treat fellow-Christians as our peers in caring is of course one reason that the professional status of pastors is often called into question by other helping disciplines. I would prefer, however, to see this as a prophetic statement to other professions which tend to diminish or dismiss the contribution of ordinary people, volunteers, because they may not have special training or receive professional levels of remuneration. In fact this peership within the Christian community is one way in which a Christian professional can find the mutual or symmetric relationships needed to maintain emotional and spiritual balance.

In relationship with other professionals the professional pastor contributes a number of distinctive emphases. A pastoral perspective will for a start be wholistic, recognizing that physical, mental, social and spiritual aspects of need are interdependent and should be treated together. Pastoral care will also emphasize the need for care to be centred on a person, making provision for individual perceptions and needs, offering a mutual relationship in which that person can be encouraged to live and grow, not just receive treatment. A pastoral perspective underlines the link between spirituality and vocation. Contained within our vocational choice and the way we exercise our professional skills are significant spiritual commitments about the place of power, status and possessions in our lives. So it is not enough to make a vocational choice and develop professional skills. We still need to understand who we are in making that choice, and decide how the skills will be used. Pastoral care has a particular perspective on what are legitimate and illegitimate uses of power: legitimate power enables and serves; illegitimate power takes advantage of weakness and seeks to control. It is not always easy to distinguish accurately between them. Pastoral care should also bring to professional dialogue an appropriate scepticism about structures and strategies. This is part of our prophetic heritage which questions any commitment to an institution, a particular method, an ideology, above a commitment to people. It places questions of justice alongside compassion in care.

Thus the pastor's contribution to the task of creating community among professionals is not a simple one. It involves confrontation as well as co-operation. It cannot be based on an unquestioning assumption of other professionals' values, strategies and institutional structures – community could not be fashioned from such a stance in any case. To claim and exercise professional peership will mean neither conformity nor alienation, but an at-times-uneasy stance which will require mature self-understanding and significant support from other pastoral colleagues. Yet at the same time peership with other professionals is essential to a pastoral vision. The wholistic thrust of pastoral care will wish to encourage and nurture integration of the approaches and insights of the many disciplines which seek to care for people. Pastoral care does not do this by attempting to lord it over these other disciplines, but by serving them. It helps to create from interdisciplinary dialogue a shared understanding of care which illuminates and affirms the contribution of each discipline as well as allocating to it a place in relation to all the others.

I began this section looking at the impact of professionalism on pastoral practice. In ending it I am moving towards suggesting ways in which a pastoral perspective might contribute to the reform of our present systems of professionalized care. It may seem presumptuous to do this, yet upon reflection I believe it is justifiable, even if only from the standpoint that members of other professional disciplines seem quite prepared to put forward their visions for reform, so why should pastoral care not do this too? More pertinently, however, it should be remembered that our present caring system has its roots in the values and methods of the pastoral tradition of the church. To explore pastoral dimensions of contemporary care is thus to offer a radical critique in the correct sense of this term – a critique from fundamentals. I have attempted to do just that throughout this book, but wish to conclude with some remarks about the purpose of care in the pastoral tradition and the implications this might have for contemporary care.

Care as creating community

Pastoral care is made up of attitudes and actions which create and maintain community. Thus care is expressed not only in healing, guiding, supporting and reconciling of individuals, but also in proper (that is, just) organization which allows each individual within a community to find a place and exercise an appropriate responsibility. Care not only nurtures and restores, but also calls individuals to opportunity and accountability within society. If I was to select one aspect of the tradition which has been most neglected in contemporary models of care – pastoral and otherwise – it would be this; that care should be directed towards creating and sustaining community.

Contemporary care is characterized by fragmentation. Stark contrasts are drawn between 'expert' care by professionals and the 'amateur' care of family, neighbours or volunteer helpers. Professional care in turn divides itself into specialties and sub-specialties which focus specific aspects of people's problems, but do so with inadequate reference to each other, making it well nigh impossible for people to gain an overview of their situation and the possibilities they face within it. Care is seldom provided in the home but rather is offered in an institutional setting, and this serves to separate care even more from everyday situations and relationships. To receive care from professional helpers removes you from the effective support of your community; to opt for the care of your community as a priority means a drastic reduction in the professional services to which you can have access.

These and similar inadequacies in care have been highlighted throughout the preceding discussion of terminal care. Clearly much of what is inadequate in terminal care is inadequate in care in general: the situation of dying people simply throws the problems into starker relief. But the question I wish to address briefly in closing is this: can a pastoral perspective suggest directions for the renewal of contemporary caring structures as well as point to their inadequacies? I believe that it can, and that stressing that care should create community would focus renewal in a number of important ways. It should help us to revise goals and methods of care, introduce values and questions of meaning in a constructive sense, and thus find new criteria to evaluate the effectiveness of the care that is offered.

To see care as creating community immediately places care in a context. No longer can it be seen simply in terms of giving a person short-term attention in order to rectify a specific problem. It is also a contribution towards equipping people for responsible membership of family and society, aiding them to find their place in their community. While care will frequently begin with response to a person's illness or crisis, a specific problem, it will also invite that person to reflect upon and assess life and its directions in the light of the problem, to take the opportunity of making a life review. Thus care nurtures personal and social development. To understand this enables us to move away from some of the difficulties inherent in our professional stance. When we isolate care from everyday life, as is our current practice, we are forced to find meaning for our caring acts in isolation. No wonder that cure, a solution to the perceived problem, becomes the desired outcome and anything else is largely unacceptable to us. Because we have isolated a person from his everyday context and committed ourselves to change a condition expressed in particular symptoms, we can only measure success or failure in terms of the persistence or disappearance of those symptoms. We cannot see how our involvement with the person might change his life in significant ways apparently unrelated to the symptoms and treatment we have offered, or how the very act of entering treatment may have triggered a renewal of relationships among his community, irrespective of the outcome of that treatment. Because the context of treatment is limited, so is our perception of what is worthwhile in care. Our fulfilment as professionals becomes invested in achieving solutions or cures; we cannot see or are unable to value the broader impact of our care.

The shift in values required if professionals are to feel fulfilled in providing terminal care illustrates this. Some professionals simply cannot find any fulfilment in working with patients or clients who cannot be cured. Others are able to broaden their understanding of care. They find fulfilment in assisting a dying person to live as fully as possible for the time that remains, helping the family to become a supportive community for the dying person and one another. While these professionals do not reject cure as a desirable outcome for illness in general, they do not require it in order to feel that their work is worthwhile. They can see their care contributing to the growth of a person and family, even though that growth is tested by shared suffering and imminent loss.

When our understanding of care is broadened to see a person's crisis or health problem in the context of her everyday life and relationships, questions of meaning arise naturally. We no longer ask only what we must do to alleviate these symptoms or cure the underlying condition. We also ask what this illness, this crisis, means for this person at this time of her life, in this network of relationships. Does the illness contain a message which has not been heard when confronted in other, less drastic, forms? Is the objective problem, the illness, itself a sign or symptom of a deeper subjective, spiritual issue which must be confronted if wholeness is to be pursued? What are the relationship issues which must be renegotiated in the light of this situation? What are the options for the future? How are the members of this person's community coping? Is their inability to cope a precipitating reason for her illness? If we are prepared to explore questions like this, even initiate them with the person in some way, then quite routine acts of care can have a profound effect on the lives of that person and her community. The interruption of everyday patterns caused by the crisis or illness becomes an opportunity for review and for some new beginnings.

To participate in or initiate a discussion of issues like these means stepping outside the boundaries of an ordinary professional relationship. It is really no one's 'job' to pick up these questions. Perhaps a chaplain might do so, although many chaplains also prefer to remain strictly within their recognized professional speciality of word and sacrament. Yet if care is to be consciously linked with growth questions like these must be confronted. Proper care needs to raise them. It should however be clear by now that I am not advocating that a professional carer *answer* those questions. Only the person can do that. But to raise the issues, to offer support in working at them, to model some ways of working with them, is a contribution which can be made by any professional who wants to add a pastoral dimension to his or her work.

A focus on care as creating community will have significant impact upon the focus of care and upon work organization. Institutional approaches to care must come under question, for these provide care largely divorced from a person's community while offering little alternative support to substitute for it. This is not to say that institutional care must be done away with. There is a case for institutional in-patient care for a variety of short-term acute care situations. But chronic care is a different matter, and we need to be committing ourselves as a society towards domiciliary forms of care in preference to institutional forms in this area. Related to this is the need for caring systems to remain relatively small and stable, so that the people involved can know each other and relate as real people rather than through their roles as professionals or patients as happens in a large hierarchical system. Work thus needs to be organized so that there is continuity of contact between helpers and patients, and so that helpers provide a healthy model of community in the way they interact with one another as well as with patients and their families. The importance and the challenge of team work has already been examined and need not be elaborated upon again. Suffice it to say that if we cannot find a way around the difficulties which inhibit team work among professionals there is little hope of professional care being able to foster community among others.

It seems to me, however, that there are signs of new directions in health care consistent with the sorts of values I have been espousing here. As yet these signs are small and preliminary, but they are signs of hope. Even the increasing number of negative critiques of our health care system and methods of professional practice is evidence that alternatives are being sought. More positively we see movements like hospice care and community health services exploring alternatives to institutionalization, endeavouring to deal with people in the context of their everyday lives. We see renewed interest in interdisciplinary dialogue. We see new programmes which understand health as positive participation in life rather than just the absence of disease. We see an increased awareness of the limitations as well as of the possibilities of medical technology. These initiatives are emerging not according to some overall master plan, but as evidences of a change in consciousness which is taking place in at least some individuals in society and among some health care professionals.

For these new directions to take root and grow a great deal more research, education and political action is required. But fundamentally what is needed is more people to become involved in a journey of self-discovery as helpers, searching out new directions, exploring alternatives. In this sense a renewed understanding and practice of health care depends upon each one of us learning to reflect upon our personal and professional lives, finding our community and working within it, committing ourselves to everyday mutual relationships which will confront our illusions yet support our exploring. We will need to face our finitude and impotence as well as our power, our helplessness as well as our hope, to uncover and meditate upon the values by which we live and out of which we offer care. Changed structures have their beginnings in changed people.

APPENDIX: REFLECTION EXERCISES

1. Seeing my own death

Settle down, make yourself comfortable, and begin to imagine your dying time. Try to build up as detailed a picture as you can. Ask yourself questions like these:

How old am I?
Where am I?
What time of day is it?
What do I see as I look around me?
What sounds, smells are there in the room or place?
What have I been doing with my life just before this time?
Who is with me?
What are they saying to me?
What do I want to say to them?

You might like to write your answers to these questions, along with any other important aspects of your dying which aren't dealt with here. You might simply like to draw the scene rather than put it into words. Or you might be content to form it and retain it in your mind's eye.

Having set the scene, reflect on the picture which has emerged for you. What significant feelings did this exercise awake in you? What resistances did you discover within yourself? What insights do you gain concerning your attitude to yourself, your values, the people you love, your hopes, your fears? How can you use these feelings and insights in caring for other people who are dying?

Think about this for a while. Often what we imagine for ourselves is our idea of an appropriate or good death. How will we cope if our dying is in fact other than 'good'? Can we accept the fact that what might be good for us might be quite unacceptable for someone else?

What does this say about the sort of care we should offer to dying people?

2. *My experience of loss*

Who we are as people and as helpers depends at least in part on our ability to experience, cope with, and grow through loss. An unwillingness to accept any more losses in our life can halt our growth as persons. An inability to come to terms with our actual and anticipated loss can lead to such painful resonances as we enter another person's story that our helping work is distorted and mainly self-protective.

Coming to terms with loss involves reflecting upon our life story, identifying the points of loss, and recognizing how we have been shaped by them. This recognition, along with the courage to re-enter and claim those losses as part of our journey, can enable us to grow as persons and as helpers.

The losses of life are various. Sometimes our principal loss is the loss of innocence, of certain illusions about ourselves and the world. At other times it is the loss of people on whom we depend, be it through death, through relocation, or through disillusionment. Other losses are those associated with growth: putting away childish things and beginning to think and feel as responsible adults; learning to accept the limitations of illness, handicap, or age. Others again come through changes in our physical circumstances, such as a new school, a new church, a new home, a new country.

The following questions are an invitation to you to enter into reflection upon your own story of loss and what it means for you. The questions are presented as a journal exercise. That is, it is suggested that reflections be written down as they come, for this written discipline is helpful in clarifying thoughts and allowing an overview to emerge. However, if you do not feel comfortable with this approach, the questions can be taken as a meditation exercise.

List some of the losses you have experienced in your life, together with your central feelings and thoughts about each one.

How have these experiences shaped your present attitudes to and feelings about life? What have you learned from them?

Have there been gains associated with the losses? How were the loss and the gain connected?

What losses do you anticipate as your life continues to unfold? Which do you fear most? How do you expect to cope? Are there ways in which you can prepare for these eventualities?

In the experience of loss, what meaning shapes and sustains you?

3. *What do I really believe?*

All of us affirm certain values, although the values we actually live by are not always the ones we say we live by, nor is our commitment in practice always as obvious as we think it is. The questions below give a way of checking on how consistently we live out the major values or beliefs of our lives. As examples, being a Christian, being a helpful person, or being a good mother, are all values which we can check in this way. Note that the questions are linked together to form a process of valuing. Each stage builds upon the previous one.

Choose a value important to you, and ask yourself the following questions. You should be able to describe decisions and actions which support your answer to each question. If you can't, then that is the place to stop and think again. Why have I missed out this stage? Is this the reason that later stages are not as firmly established as I would like them to be? What should I do to strengthen my valuing or believing at this point?

Choosing:
1. Did I choose this value freely?
2. Was I aware of alternatives?
3. Did I carefully consider the consequences of those alternatives?

Prizing:
4. Am I happy with my choice?
5. Am I willing to affirm it publicly?

Acting:
6. Am I acting upon my choice?
7. Are my actions consistent, forming a pattern of life?

4. *A reflection on personal power*

Frequently we as helpers are reluctant or unwilling to acknowledge our influence or power over other people's lives. Yet the very act of refusing to accept that we have power can result in us abusing it. If we do not recognize our importance to other people we may place enormous pressure upon them through 'friendly advice' or hurt them deeply because of the off-handedness or unpredictability we bring to the relationship.

Learning about our power will involve us in a consideration of our own needs, our responses to other people, and their responses to us. Some useful questions to reflect upon are:

What are the areas of life in which I need to maintain control? In what ways does this affect my relationship with others?

Do I understand myself principally in terms of my job? Am I more comfortable when I can operate in a given role or when I can just be myself?

Which people attract me? Repel me? What does this say about the unrecognized or unadmitted (shadow) part of myself? How do I respond to people who try to organize me or give me advice? On what issues and in what ways do I seek to influence others? Who are the people before whom I feel powerless? Do I have authorities whom I feel I cannot question?

What keeps me from acting on my dreams or ambitions?

Who are the members of my community? How do other people experience me? From my observation? From their comments? From their actions?

Is this consistent with the way I see and feel about myself? How can I and they achieve a more appropriate perception of each other?

Reading for further reflection might include:

Adolf Guggenbühl-Craig, *Power in the Helping Professions*, Spring, Dallas 1982.
Rollo May, *Power and Innocence*, Norton, New York 1972.
Claude Steiner, *The Other Side of Power*, Grove, New York 1981.

Exercises 1, 2 and 3 from B. D. Rumbold, *Living with Cancer: a video workbook*, Baptist Union of Victoria, Melbourne 1985. Used with permission.

NOTES

1 Terminal Care Today

1. Talcott Parsons, Renee C. Fox and Victor M. Lidz, 'The "Gift of Life" and its Reciprocation', *Social Research*, *39*, 1972, pp. 365–415.
2. Elisabeth Kübler-Ross, *On Death and Dying*, Macmillan, New York 1969; Tavistock Press 1970.
3. Carl Nighswonger, 'Ministry to the Dying as a Learning Encounter', *Journal of Thanatology, 1*, 1971, pp. 101–108.
4. Sudnow goes further, demonstrating that the quality of care which a patient gets is dependent on how significant and interesting that patient appears to the staff. The predominantly middle-class staff tend to see lower-class patients as less interesting and less deserving. David Sudnow, *Passing On: the social organization of dying*, Prentice-Hall, NJ 1967.
5. Peritz Levinson, 'Obstacles in the Treatment of Dying Patients', *American Journal of Psychiatry, 132*, 1975, pp. 28–32.
6. Bernard Schoenberg, Arthur Carr, Austin Kutscher, David Peretz and Ivan Goldberg (eds), *Anticipatory Grief*, Columbia University Press, New York 1974.
7. Austin Kutscher, 'Anticipatory Grief, Death and Bereavement: A Continuum', in Edith Wyschogrod (ed), *The Phenomenon of Death: Faces of Mortality*, Harper Colophon, New York 1973, pp. 40–53.
8. See for example the conclusions reached by Cartwright et al in their study of the final year of life of 960 randomly-selected people in 12 different regions of England and Wales. Ann Cartwright, Lisbeth Hockey and John Anderson, *Life before Death*, Routledge and Kegan Paul 1973, pp. 184–185.
9. Michael Wilson, *The Hospital – a place of truth*, University of Birmingham Institute for the study of worship and religious architecture, 1971, pp. 1–56 in particular.
10. Herman Feifel, Susan Hanson, Robert Jones and Lauri Edwards, 'Physicians consider Death'. *Proceedings, 75th Annual Convention, American Psychological Association*, American Psychological Association, Washington DC, 1967, pp. 201–202. Further discussion of this study is to be found in Herman Feifel, 'Perception of Death', *Annals of the New York Academy of Sciences, 164* (art. 3), 1969, pp. 669–674. Also in Herman Feifel, 'Religious conviction and fear of death among the healthy and terminally-ill', *Journal for the Scientific Study of Religion, 13*, 1974, pp. 353–360.

11. See for example Jeanne Quint, *The Nurse and the Dying Patient*, Macmillan, New York 1967.

12. Glaser and Strauss' work was commissioned by the Nursing Research Council of the National Institute of Health, Washington DC, and has been published in four volumes: Barney Glaser and Anselm Strauss, *Awareness of Dying: a sociological study of attitudes toward patients dying in hospitals*, Weidenfeld & Nicholson 1965. Barney Glaser and Anselm Strauss, *Time for Dying*, Aldine Press, Chicago 1968. Jeanne Quint, op. cit. Anselm Strauss and Barney Glaser, *Anguish: a case history of a dying trajectory*, The Sociology Press, Mill Valley, CA 1970.

13. A description more sympathetic to the staff's position is given by Jim McIntosh, *Communication and Awareness in a Cancer Ward*, Croom Helm 1977.

14. See for example Adriaan Verwoerdt, *Communication with the Fatally Ill*, Charles C. Thomas, Springfield 1966.

15. Sandol Stoddard, *The Hospice Movement: a better way of caring for the dying*, Jonathan Cape 1979.

2 Helping and Helplessness

1. See for example the observations of Kübler-Ross, *On Death and Dying*, p. 254.

2. Sigmund Freud, *Inhibitions, Symptoms and Anxiety*, Complete Psychological Works Vol 20, 1925–26, Hogarth Press, pp. 161ff.

3. For example see J. Sartre, *Being and Nothingness*, Washington Square Press, New York 1966; M. Heidegger, *Being and Time*, Blackwell 1967.

4. Martin E. P. Seligman, *Helplessness: on depression, development and death*, Freeman-Scribners, San Francisco 1975. Seligman is both an experimental and clinical psychologist whose interests include learning theory and motivational research. Unless otherwise noted, the material on Seligman's research presented in this chapter is drawn from this reference.

5. Ibid., p. 47.

6. This hypothesis of an intermediate state between information about a situation (Stimulus) and the behaviour resulting from that information (Response) has set off a considerable debate among learning theorists. It is of course a fundamental challenge to Stimulus-Response models of learning, and it would seem that even if alternative explanations of Seligman's data are forthcoming the S-R models will not survive unchanged. For an introduction to this debate see: Steven F. Maier and Martin E. P. Seligman, 'Learned Helplessness: theory and evidence', *Journal of Experimental Psychology: General*, *105*, 1976, pp. 3–46, and the critique by Donald J. Levis, 'Learned Helplessness: a reply and an alternative S-R interpretation', *Journal of Experimental Psychology: General*, *105*, 1976, pp. 47–65.

7. David C. Klein, Ellen Fencil-Morse and Martin E. P. Seligman, 'Learned Helplessness, Depression, and the Attribution of Failure', *Journal of Personality and Social Psychology*, *33*, 1976, pp. 508–516.

8. For a comprehensive review see Herbert M. Lefcourt, *Locus of Control: current trends in theory and research*, Lawrence Erlbaum Associates, New York 1976.

9. Ibid., p. 148.

10. Seligman, *Helplessness*, Chapter 5.

11. Robert Ardrey, *The Territorial Imperative*, Atheneum, New York 1966.

12. Robert W. White, 'Motivation Reconsidered: the concept of competence', *Psychological Review, 66*, 1959, pp. 297–333; 'Ego and Reality in Psychoanalytical Theory: a proposal regarding independent ego energies', *Psychological Issues*, Monograph II, 1963.

13. Maslow argues that the need to know is a universal human phenomenon, perhaps with an instinct-like nature. Associated with it however is also fear of that knowledge. Knowledge may sometimes be avoided through a desire to escape responsibility or through a failure of courage. But in general humans prefer to see reality as it is, even if it hurts. Abraham Maslow, 'The Need to Know and the Fear of Knowing', *Journal of General Psychology, 68*, 1963, pp. 111–125. Maslow's statement is of course of particular relevance to those with an internal locus of control.

14. Within an institution a patient may be regarded virtually as a symptom-vehicle, with medical attention focussed on the symptoms rather than on the person who exhibits them. This attitude is reflected in and reinforced by the language of the hospital, with disease and even the patient's body parts referred to impersonally, implicitly dissociated from the person involved. Such language and attitudes readily lead to patients seeing themselves as depersonalized. See for further reference Eric J. Cassell, 'Disease as an "It": concepts of disease revealed by patients' presentation of symptoms', *Social Science and Medicine, 10*, 1976, pp. 143–146; Anna Baziak and Robert Dentan. 'The Language of the Hospital and its effects on the Patient', in James K. Skinner and Robert C. Leonard (eds), *Social Interaction and Patient Care*, J. P. Lippincott, Philadelphia 1965, pp. 272–277.

15. Lawrence LeShan, 'Psychotherapy and the Dying Patient', in Leonard Pearson (ed), *Death and Dying: current issues in the treatment of the dying person*, Case Western Reserve University Press, Cleveland 1969.

16. Ann Cartwright, *Patients and their Doctors: a study of General Practice*, Routledge and Kegan Paul 1967.

17. David E. Hayes-Bautista, 'Modifying the treatment: patient compliance, patient control, and medical care', *Social Science and Medicine, 10*, 1976, pp. 233–238; Elihu M. Gerson, 'The Social Character of Illness: deviance or politics?', *Social Science and Medicine, 10*, 1976, pp. 219–224.

18. Jean Comaroff, 'Communicating information about non-fatal illness: the strategies of a group of general practitioners', *Sociological Review, 24*, 1976, pp. 269–290. Data concerning doctors' strategies for terminal illness indicates that here more doctors are likely to adopt a stereotyped or controlling role.

19. See for example Ronald J. Burke and Tamara Weir, 'Personality characteristics associated with giving and receiving help', *Psychological Reports, 38*, 1976, pp. 343–353; Hugh Eadie, 'The Helping Personality', *Contact, 49*, 1975, pp. 2–17.

20. For a critique of transference as a rationalization and avoidance of appropriate responsibility in a helping relationship see Liam Hudson, *Human Beings: an introduction to the psychology of human experience*, Jonathan Cape 1975, p. 177.

21. K. R. Eissler, *The Psychiatrist and the Dying Patient*, International Universities Press, New York 1955, pp. 243–250.

22. Ibid., p. 250.

23. See for example Andrew Samuels, *Jung and the Post-Jungians*, Routledge & Kegan Paul 1985, pp. 173–176; Madeleine Davis and David

Wallbridge, *Boundary and Space: an introduction to the work of D. W. Winnicott*, Penguin 1983. A detailed discussion of the analytic relationship in similar terms is given by Patrick Casement, *On Learning from the Patient*, Tavistock Press 1985.

24. Sidney M. Jourard, *The Transparent Self*, Van Nostrand Reinhold, New York 1964; revised edition 1971.

25. Bill L. Kell and William J. Mueller, *Impact and Change: a study of counselling relationships*, Appleton-Century-Crofts, New York 1966. See also Rollo May, 'On the Phenomenological Bases of Psychotherapy' in Nathaniel Lawrence and Daniel O'Connor (eds), *Readings in Existential Phenomenology*, Prentice Hall, Englewood Cliffs, NJ 1967, pp. 365–376; Jerome D. Frank, *Persuasion and Healing: a comparative study of psychotherapy*, Schocken Books, New York 1961; revised edition 1974, pp. 194–198.

26. David H. Clark, *Social Therapy in Psychiatry*, Penguin 1974.

3. Pastoral Perspectives

1. Wayne E. Oates, *New Dimensions in Pastoral Care*, Fortress Press, Philadelphia 1970, p. 3.

2. Eduard Thurneysen, *A Theology of Pastoral Care*, John Knox Press, Richmond, VA 1962, pp. 52f.

3. Recently Alastair Campbell has followed a similar approach in his useful and stimulating book: Alastair Campbell, *Rediscovering Pastoral Care*, Darton, Longman & Todd 1981.

4. F. F. Bruce, *This is That: the New Testament development of some Old Testament themes*, Paternoster Press 1968, p. 100.

5. Seward Hiltner, *Preface to Pastoral Theology*, Abingdon Press, Nashville 1958, pp. 89–172. William Clebsch and Charles Jaekle, *Pastoral Care in Historical Perspective: an essay with exhibits*, Harper Torch Books, New York 1967, p. 4.

6. Ezek. 34.23f. The same theme of the shepherd-king recurs in Zech. 9–14, and it is these prophecies which are used as an interpretative background to the New Testament passion narratives, showing Jesus to be the fulfilment of these hopes: Bruce, op cit., pp. 101–114.

7. Raymond E. Brown, *The Gospel according to John*, Doubleday & Co, New York 1966, Volume 1, pp. 395–398.

8. Ibid., p. 398.

9. See 1 Peter 5.2, 1 Tim. 4.12–5.2, I Cor. 16.15, I Thess. 5.12, Heb. 13.17, Gal. 6.2, Col. 3.12–17, Matt. 5.43–48, I Thess. 3.12.

10. Clebsch and Jaekle, op. cit., pp. 11–30.

11. Walther Zimmerli and Joachim Jeremias, *The Servant of God*, SCM Press 1957.

12. James Luther Mays, *Ezekiel, Second Isaiah*, Fortress Press, Philadelphia 1978, pp. 84–91.

13. Zimmerli and Jeremias, op. cit., p. 93ff.

14. Ibid., p. 104.

15. Reginald H. Fuller, *The Foundations of New Testament Christology*, Collins 1969, p. 130.

16. Oscar Cullman, *The Christology of the New Testament* (revised edition), SCM Press 1963, pp. 66f.

17. Anthony T. Hanson, *The Church of the Servant*, SCM Press 1962.

18. Donald G. Dawe, *The Form of a Servant: an historical analysis of the kenotic motif*, Fortress Press, Philadelphia 1963.

19. J. A. T. Robinson, *The Human Face of God*, SCM Press and Westminister Press 1972, pp. 207f.

20. P. T. Forsyth, *The Person and the Place of Jesus Christ* (1909), Eerdmans, Grand Rapids, pp. 291–357 in particular. C. F. D. Moule, 'The Manhood of Jesus in the New Testament', in S. W. Sykes and J. P. Clayton (eds), *Christ, Faith and History: Cambridge Studies in Christology*, CUP 1972, pp. 95–110.

21. Eduard Schweizer, *The Good News according to Matthew*, SPCK 1976, p. 62.

22. T. Ralph Morton, *Jesus: Man for Today*, Abingdon Press, Nashville 1970.

23. Henri Nouwen, *The Wounded Healer*, Doubleday & Co, New York 1972, pp. 94f. See also the discussion in Campbell, op. cit., pp. 37–46.

24. See for example Michael Wilson's description of the medical model of care in Michael Wilson, *Health is for People*, Darton, Longman & Todd 1975, pp. 1–32.

25. For example: Ivan Illich, *Medical Nemesis: the expropriation of health*, Calder & Boyars 1975; Ivan Illich, Irving Zola, John McKnight, Jonathan Caplan and Harley Shaiken, *Disabling Professions*, Marion Boyars 1977.

4. Hope

1. Kübler-Ross, *On Death and Dying*, p. 139.

2. Avery Weisman, *On Dying and Denying: a psychiatric study of terminality*, Behavioural Publications, New York 1972.

3. Ibid., p. 67.

4. See for example Verwoerdt, *Communication with the Fatally Ill*, Chapter 2; Weisman, op. cit., pp. 69f.

5. Some examples are to be found in Liston O. Mills, 'Pastoral Care of the Dying and Bereaved', in Liston Mills (ed), *Perspectives on Death*, Abingdon, Nashville 1969, pp. 253–282, pp. 258f.; Kübler-Ross, *On Death and Dying*, pp. 114–119, 174–176; Avery Weisman and Thomas Hackett, 'Predilection to Death', in Robert Fulton (ed), *Death and Identity*, Wiley, New York 1965, pp. 293–329, pp. 306f.

6. Martin Heidegger, *Being and Time*, Blackwell 1967, pp. 281–293 in particular.

7. Recently John Macquarrie has made a similar distinction in his useful discussion of hope in his *Christian Hope*, Mowbray 1978.

8. Erikson calls this totalism, occurring when part of existence is treated as if it were the whole. Erik Erikson, *Identity: Youth and Crisis*, Faber & Faber 1968, p. 81. A similar dynamic in cases of mental illness is described by William Lynch, *Images of Hope: imagination as healer of the hopeless*, University of Notre Dame Press 1974.

9. Oscar Cullman, 'Immortality of the Soul or Resurrection of the Dead?' (1958) in Krister Stendahl (ed), *Immortality and Resurrection*, Macmillan, New York 1965, pp. 9–53.

10. Jürgen Moltmann, *Theology of Hope*, SCM Press 1967.

11. For a symposium involving thinkers from all three positions see Ewert Cousins (ed), *Hope and the Future of Man*, Fortress Press, Philadelphia 1972.

12. For example, Charles Hartshorne, *A Natural Theology for our Time*, Open Court, La Salle, Ill., 1967, p. 56. It is interesting to note that while Hartshorne

defends this sense of continuing contribution as the essential content of hope, Lifton contends that it is precisely the breakdown of this sort of hope by the threat of nuclear holocaust which has precipitated the present spiritual crisis. Robert Jay Lifton, *Boundaries: psychological man in revolution*, Random House, New York 1967.

13. Graeme Griffin, *Death and the Church: problems and possibilities*, Dove Communications, Melbourne 1978, pp. 7f.

14. Wolfhart Pannenberg, *Jesus – God and Man*, SCM Press and Westminster Press 1968, pp. 84–88.

15. Macquarrie's final chapter (Macquarrie, op. cit., pp. 106–127) is an interesting, although somewhat speculative, exploration of this tension.

16. See Paul's account of his priorities in Phil. 1.21–26.

17. See for example Luke 9.23, II Cor. 4.11.

5. Dying Well

1. Robert Kastenbaum, 'Towards standards of care for the terminally ill, Part II: What standards exist today?', *Omega, The Journal of Death and Dying*, 6, 1975, pp. 289–90.

2. Talcott Parsons et al, for example, argue that current medical attitudes can be traced directly to the Judaeo-Christian emphasis on the gift of life by God, and the reciprocation required of man. Talcott Parsons, Renee C. Fox, and Victor M. Lidz. 'The "Gift of Life" and its Reciprocation', *Social Research*, 39, 1972, pp. 365–415. This article clearly emphasizes continuity. The discontinuity between a religious world view and modern clinical medicine is described by Michel Foucault, *The Birth of the Clinic; an archeology of medical perception*, Tavistock Press 1973.

3. II Sam. 14.14. 'We must all die: we are like water spilt on the ground that can never be gathered up again' (JB). See also Pss. 6.5, 30.9, 88.10–12, 115.17, Isa. 38.11.

4. Deut. 30.15–20, Ezek. 3.18ff.

5. Pss. 49.7–10, 73.2ff., 92.7f.

6. Rudolf Bultmann with G. von Rad and G. Bertram, *Life and Death*, A. and C. Black 1965, p. 44.

7. Ibid., p. 51.

8. Leander E. Keck, 'New Testament Views of Death', in Mills (ed), *Perspectives on Death*, pp. 33–98.

9. For example, Luke 13.1–5.

10. II Tim. 1.10, I Tim. 2.11, Rom. 6.5f., I Thess. 4.16, I Cor. 15.18.

11. Jaroslav Pelikan, *The Shape of Death: life, death and immortality in the Early Fathers*, Abingdon Press, Nashville 1961, pp. 11–29.

12. Ibid., pp. 33–52.

13. Ibid., pp. 55–73.

14. Milton McC. Gatch, 'Some Theological Reflections on Death from the Early Church through the Reformation', in Mills (ed), *Perspectives on Death*, pp. 99–136.

15. Philippe Aries, *Western Attitudes toward Death from the Middle Ages to the Present*, Marion Boyars 1976, p. 33.

16. T. S. R. Boase, *Death in the Middle Ages: mortality, judgement and remembrance*, Thames and Hudson 1972. J. Huizinga, *The Waning of the Middle Ages*, Doubleday Anchor, New York 1954, pp. 138–151.

17. Anon., *Ars Moriendi* (c. 1450). Excerpt in Clebsch and Jaekle, op. cit., pp. 178–189, p. 180.

18. Aries, op. cit., pp. 11f.

19. Ibid., p. 37.

20. Martin Luther, 'The Fourteenth of Consolation' (1520). Excerpt in Clebsch and Jaekle, op. cit., pp. 211–223.

21. John Calvin, Letters (1541–1549), 'To William Farel, To Farel, and To Madame de Cany', Reprinted in Clebsch and Jaekle, op. cit., pp. 226–232.

22. Aries, op. cit., p. 38.

23. Jeremy Taylor, *Holy Living and Dying* (1651), George Bell 1875, p. 387.

24. Ibid., pp. 294f.

25. Ibid., p. 502.

26. David E. Stannard, 'Death and Dying in Puritan New England', *American Historical Review*, 78, 1973, pp. 1305–1330. (For a fuller account see Stannard, *The Puritan Way of Death*, Oxford University Press, New York 1977).

27. Ibid., p. 1317.

28. William Ward, 'An Address from the Baptist Missionaries in India, to the Hindoos', *Massachusetts Baptist Missionary Magazine*, *1*, 1803, pp. 27–31, p. 30.

29. Michel Foucault, *The Birth of the Clinic; an archeology of medical perception*, Tavistock Press 1973.

30. Marie-Francoise-Xavier Bichat, *Anatomie Generale*, 1803, p. xcix. Quoted by Foucault, ibid., p. 146.

31. Carl Friedrich Marx, 'Medical Euthanasia' (1826), translated by Walter Cane, *Journal of the History of Medicine*, 7, 1952, pp. 401–416, p. 410.

32. Philippe Aries, *The Hour of our Death*, Penguin 1983, pp. 559–601.

33. See for example: J. Gordon Cox (ed), *A Priest's Work in Hospital: a handbook for Hospital Chaplains and other of the clergy who visit hospitals*, SPCK 1955, pp. 82–85 in particular.

34. See for example: David Cole Gordon, *Overcoming the Fear of Death*, Penguin 1972; Stanley Keleman, *Living Your Dying*, Random House, New York 1974; Martin Shepard, *Someone you love is dying: a guide for helping and coping*, Harmony Books, New York 1975.

35. As examples see: Mark Peachey, *Facing Terminal Illness*, Herald Press, Scottdale 1981; David Watson, *Fear No Evil. a personal struggle with cancer*, Hodder & Stoughton 1984.

36. Ladislaus Boros, *The Moment of Truth: mysterium mortis*, Search Press 1965.

37. Roger Troisfontaines, *I do not die*, Deselee, New York 1963.

38. Alfred North Whitehead, *Process and Reality*, Macmillan, New York 1929.

39. Charles Hartshorne, *A Natural Theology for Our Time*, Open Court, La Salle, Ill 1967.

40. Robert A. Lambourne, 'Hospital Salt, Theological Savour, and True Humanism', a paper given at the Consultation on Health and Salvation, Tübingen 1967. Reprinted in *Explorations in Health and Salvation: a selection of papers by Bob Lambourne*, Institute for the Study of Worship and Religious Architecture, Birmingham 1983.

41. Michael Wilson, *Health is for People*, Darton, Longman & Todd 1975, p. 28.

42. This is the definition used in Lord Raglan's Bill concerning euthanasia, debated in the House of Lords in March 1969.

43. London Medical Group and the Society for the Study of Medical Ethics, 'The Problem of Euthanasia', *Contact, 38*, 1972, Supplement; General Synod Board for Social Responsibility, *On Dying Well: an Anglican contribution to the debate on euthanasia*, CIO 1975.

44. Weisman, *On Dying and Denying*, pp. 39f.

45. Elisabeth Kübler-Ross (ed), *Death: the final stage of growth*, Prentice-Hall, NJ 1975.

46. See Weisman's contributions to the discussion in an extended case study, 'The Question of an Appropriate Death' in Avery D. Weisman, *The Realization of Death*, Jason Aronson, New York 1974, pp. 138–152.

47. Paul Ramsey, 'The Indignity of "Death with Dignity" ', *Hastings Center Studies, 2*, 1974, pp. 47–62. Ramsey suggests that much of the idea of dignity in dying is a projection of the feelings of nobility and dignity in caring for the dying, rather than an observation concerning dying itself. This suggestion appears to have some support from professional helpers' reactions to death: death is appropriate if it proceeds according to staff expectations, inappropriate if it does not. The idea is staff – rather than patient – centred.

48. Ps. 90.12; Ps. 39.4–6.

49. This process of faithful living is set out in Rom. 12.

6. Better Terminal Care

1. Evelyn E. and James D. Whitehead, *Community of Faith: models and strategies for Developing Christian Communities*, Seabury, New York 1982, pp. 21–33.

2. Rosalie A. Kane, 'The Interprofessional Team as a Small Group', *Social Work in Health Care, 1*, 1975, pp. 19–32.

3. M. de Wachter, 'Interdisciplinary Teamwork', *Journal of Medical Ethics, 2*, 1976, pp. 52–57.

4. Ibid., p. 56.

5. Samuel Klagsbrun, 'Cancer, Emotion and Nurses', *American Journal of Psychiatry, 126*, 1970, pp. 71–78.

6. Warren Kinston, 'Hospital Organization and Structure and its Effect on Inter-Professional Behaviour and the Delivery of Care', *Social Science and Medicine, 17*, 1983, pp. 1159–1170.

7. Paul M. DuBois, *The Hospice Way of Death*, Human Sciences Press, New York 1980; James Ewen and Patricia Herrington, *Hospice: a handbook for families and others facing terminal illness*, Bear & Company, Santa Fe 1983; Sandol Stoddard, *The Hospice Movement: a better way to care for the dying*, Jonathan Cape 1978.

8. Robert Buckingham, *The Complete Hospice Guide*, Harper & Row, New York 1983; Cicely Saunders, Dorothy Summers and Neville Teller (eds), *Hospice: the living idea*, Edward Arnold 1981.

9. Annual Report, St Christopher's Hospice, London, 1977–78, pp. 17–18.

10. Marjorie Sue Cox, 'The Connecticut Hospice Volunteer Program', in Hamilton and Reid (eds), *A Hospice Handbook: a new way to care for the dying*, Eerdmans, Grand Rapids 1980.

11. C. Murray Parkes and Jenny Parkes, ' "Hospice" versus "Hospital"

care – re-evaluation after 10 years as seen by surviving spouses', *Postgraduate Medical Journal, 60*, 1984, pp. 120–124.

12. Robert Kane, Jeffrey Wales, Leslie Bernstein, Arleen Leibowitz and Stevan Kaplan, 'A Randomised Controlled Trial of Hospice Care', *The Lancet*, 21 April 1984, pp. 890–896.

13. A detailed outline of the study plan has been published: David Greer, Vincent Mor, Sylvia Sherwood, John Morris and Howard Birnbaum, 'National Hospice Study Analysis Plan', *Journal of Chronic Diseases, 36*, 1983, pp. 737–780.

14. Howard Birnbaum and David Kidder, 'What Does Hospice Cost?', *American Journal of Public Health, 74*, 1984, pp. 689–697.

15. Balfour Mount and John Scott, 'Whither Hospice Evaluation' *Journal of Chronic Diseases, 36*, 1983, pp. 731–736.

16. Dunt and Cantwell: publication forthcoming.

17. It has been estimated for example that in the next decade the cancer burden in Victoria will increase by about 18%: Victorian Co-operative Oncology Group, *Palliative Care in Victoria: report of a sub-committee*, Anti-Cancer Council of Victoria, Melbourne 1984, p. 13.

18. Ibid. The recommendations of the sub-committee have since been incorporated in the *Report of the Ministerial Committee to Review Cancer Services in Victoria*, Health Department of Victoria, October 1985.

19. Eric Wilkes, 'The Hospice in Great Britain', in *Hospice: the living idea*, pp. 184–186.

20. See for example Buckingham, *The Complete Hospice Guide*, pp. 144f.; Cicely Saunders, 'Evolution in Terminal Care' in Saunders (ed), *The Management of Terminal Malignant Disease*, Edward Arnold, ²1984, pp. 213–17.

21. See reports such as *Working Party Report on Terminal Care*, HMSO 1980; *Report of the Ministerial Committee to Review Cancer Services in Victoria*.

22. David S. Greer and Vincent Mor, 'Response to a letter of Dame Cicely Saunders concerning Evaluation of Hospice Activities', *Journal of Chronic Diseases, 37*, 1984, pp. 872–873.

23. Paul Torrens, 'Achievement, failure and the future: hospice analysed', in *Hospice: the living idea*, pp. 187–194.

7. *Professional Care and Pastoral Care*

1. G. E. Millerson, *The Qualifying Associations: a study in professionalism*, Routledge & Kegan Paul 1964. Millerson reviews the work of 21 authors who list the definitive elements of a true profession. Among them 23 attributes are regarded as essential; but no single attribute is common to all 21 authors!

2. Darrell Reeck, *Ethics for the Professions: a Christian perspective*, Augsburg, Minneapolis 1982, p. 18.

3. Paul Wilding, *Professional Power and Social Welfare*, Routledge & Kegan Paul 1982.

4. Ibid., pp. 19–58.

5. For a detailed discussion of these and similar issues see Wilding, op. cit., pp. 85–128. Illich's radical critique of professional practice, *Disabling Professions*, has already been referred to. To qualify Illich's utopian stance it is appropriate to refer also to David Horrobin, *Medical Hubris: a reply to Ivan Illich*, Churchill Livingstone 1978.

6. Karen Lebacqz, *Professional Ethics: power and paradox*, Abingdon, Nashville 1985, pp. 124–136.

7. Horrobin, op. cit., pp. 16f., 106.

8. Illich, *Medical Nemesis*, p. 28.

9. Wilding, op. cit., p. 137.

10. Alastair Campbell, *Moderated Love: a theology of professional practice*, SPCK 1984.

11. Ibid., p. 126.

12. Adolf Guggenbühl-Craig, *Power in the Helping Professions*, The Analytical Psychology Club, New York 1971; Spring Publications, Dallas 1982.

13. Ibid., pp. 85–101.

14. Horrobin, op. cit., p. 102.

15. For example: Robert Lambourne, 'With Love to The USA', in Hugh Melinsky (ed), *Religion and Medicine*, SCM Press 1970; Paul Pruyser, *The Minister as Diagnostician*, Westminster, Philadelphia 1976; Charles Gerkin, *The Living Human Document: re-visioning pastoral counselling in a hermeneutical mode*, Abingdon, Nashville 1984.